DARE
TO
DREAM
AGAIN

FOREWORD BY STEVE BACKLUND

DARE TO DREAM AGAIN

Break Free from Fear, Intimidation, Unworthiness, and Step into Your God-Sized Dreams

MELINDA LAGAAY

Dare to Dream Again
Copyright © 2025
MELINDA LAGAAY

All rights reserved.

No part of this publication may be reproduced, distributed, or transmitted in any form or by any means, including photocopying, recording, or other electronic or mechanical methods, without the prior written permission of the author, except in the case of brief quotations embodied in critical reviews and certain other non-commercial uses permitted by copyright law.

MELINDA LAGAAY
Printed in the United States.
First Printing 2025
First Edition 2025
Paperback ISBN: 978-1-7378073-2-2

Edited by: Angela Parker

Scriptures marked NIV are taken from the NEW INTERNATIONAL VERSION (NIV): Scripture taken from THE HOLY BIBLE, NEW INTERNATIONAL VERSION ®. Copyright© 1973, 1978, 1984, 2011 by Biblica, Inc.™.
Used by permission of Zondervan.
Scriptures marked NKJV are taken from the NEW KING JAMES VERSION (NKJV): Scripture taken from the NEW KING JAMES VERSION®. Copyright© 1982 by Thomas Nelson, Inc. Used by permission. All rights reserved.
Scripture taken from the Amplified Bible (AMPCE), Copyright © 1954, 1958, 1962, 1964, 1965, 1987 by The Lockman Foundation. Used by permission.
Scripture quotations marked (AMPCE) are taken from the Amplified Bible, Copyright © 1954, 1958, 1962, 1964, 1965, 1987
by The Lockman Foundation. Used by permission.
Scripture taken from the Amplified Bible,
Copyright © 2015 by The Lockman Foundation.
Used by permission.
Scripture quotations marked (AMP) are taken from the Amplified Bible, Copyright © 2015 by The Lockman Foundation. Used by permission.
Scripture quotations are from The ESV® Bible (The Holy Bible, English Standard Version®), © 2001 by Crossway, a publishing ministry of Good News Publishers.
Used by permission.
All rights reserved.

TABLE OF CONTENTS

About the Author vii
Dedication ix
Acknowledgements xi
Endorsements xiii
Foreword By Steve Backlund xv

PART 1: DARE TO DREAM AGAIN

Introduction: You are Worthy of Your Dreams 1
Chapter 1   You Have an Inheritance 7
Chapter 2   Stepping Into Your God-Sized D.R.E.A.M.S 20
Chapter 3   Speak Life Over Your Dreams 32
Chapter 4   Your Generational Inheritance 43
Chapter 5   It's Time to Get Going! 50
Chapter 6   Your Work Will Be Rewarded 57
Chapter 7   Driven by Destiny 65
Chapter 8   The Power of Forgiveness to Step Into Your Dreams ... 75
Chapter 9   The Time is Now 84

PART 2 : THE DARE TO DREAM AGAIN ACTIVATIONS: PRACTICAL STEPS TO CREATE MOMENTUM, TAKE ACTION, AND STEP INTO YOUR GOD-SIZED DREAMS.

More About the Author 119
Other Books by Melinda & Pieter Lagaay 121

ABOUT THE AUTHOR

Melinda Lagaay is a true visionary who loves to build, teach, and equip the body of Christ. Melinda believes that with God, all things are possible. Melinda is a licensed pastor at Bethel Church in Redding, California. Melinda and her husband Pieter are passionate about seeing marriages restored and seeing people step into their dreams. Melinda's powerful testimony demonstrates that love conquers all and dreams can be resurrected, no matter the circumstance.

DEDICATION

I dedicate this book to my sister, Lisa Heiderick. I love that God gave me not only a sister, but a best friend! Your belief in me and support of me has brought some of the biggest breakthroughs in my life. You are a powerful prophet, and a voice of encouragement, purity, love and power, and I am grateful to be able to call you my sister and best friend! I love you!

ACKNOWLEDGEMENTS

I'm so grateful for my friend and editor, Angela Parker, whose incredible talent and heart have made *Dare to Dream Again* shine. You've been my friend and biggest supporter, cheering me on through every step of this journey. Your belief in me has been a game-changer, helping me share God's call to dream big with the world—thank you! Your encouragement and support means so much to me! I am so grateful to call you a friend and family. Thank you for the difference you've made in my life and in the lives of so many. You are more than just an editor, you are a prophetic voice of wisdom in my life, and I am blessed to know you.

ENDORSEMENTS

As Melinda's husband, I've witnessed a miracle unfold—a woman who rose from the depths of betrayal, heartbreak, and self-doubt to become a living manifestation of God's redemptive power. *Dare to Dream Again* is a masterpiece of hope, written by a woman whose authority comes from conquering the unthinkable with unyielding faith. My wife is a licensed pastor at Bethel Church and a visionary leader with Igniting Hope Ministries, who has overcome being a victim of infidelity, unworthiness, and fear to step into her God-sized dreams. Her story—our story—of a marriage restored and dreams resurrected will set your heart on fire with possibility.

Melinda's voice carries the weight of someone who's faced the enemy's lies head-on and emerged victorious. *In Dare to Dream Again*, Melinda delivers prophetic wisdom and practical tools with the conviction of a woman anointed to awaken dreamers. Every page pulses with hope, breaking off fear of failure and victim mindsets. Melinda carries an anointing to impart revelation to reimagine your story, and claim your divine inheritance.

This book is a rallying cry for every Christian woman longing to live boldly for Jesus. Melinda's powerful testimony and actionable steps will inspire you to silence intimidation, speak life over your dreams, and impact generations. *Dare to Dream Again* isn't just a read—it's an invitation to soar into the abundant life God has for you. I wholeheartedly endorse this life-changing work, believing it will ignite your faith and propel you toward your destiny. Pick up this book and let Melinda's authority and God's promises transform you!

Pieter Lagaay

FOREWORD

By Steve Backlund

I am thrilled to endorse Melinda Lagaay's powerful and inspiring book, *Dare to Dream Again*. As someone who has had the privilege of walking alongside Melinda during her transformative journey at Bethel School of Supernatural Ministry and within Igniting Hope Ministries, I can attest to the authenticity and passion that permeate every page of this book. Melinda's story is a testament to the redemptive power of God, showing how He can take a life marked by pain, fear, and feelings of unworthiness and turn it into a beacon of hope, purpose, and destiny.

This book is more than a personal narrative; it's a practical and prophetic guide for anyone who has ever felt disqualified from dreaming big with God. Melinda's vulnerability in sharing her struggles—overcoming a past filled with betrayal, self-doubt, and intimidation—creates a safe space for readers to confront their own fears and limiting beliefs. Her insights, rooted in biblical truth and hard-won experience, offer actionable steps to break free from survival mode and step boldly into God-sized dreams. Her emphasis on reimagining the past, speaking life over dreams, and embracing generational blessings is both empowering and deeply encouraging.

What sets this book apart is Melinda's heart to see others rise. Her journey from a stay-at-home mom who felt unqualified to a pastor, author, and ministry leader reflects the very principles she teaches: that no one is too broken for God to use mightily. Her stories of overcoming fear to preach, write, and lead—often with my wife, Wendy, and me cheering her on—will inspire readers to say "yes" to their own callings, no matter how impossible they seem.

I wholeheartedly recommend *Dare to Dream Again* to anyone ready to silence the enemy's lies, embrace their inheritance, and take courageous steps toward their divine purpose. Melinda's voice is a gift to this generation, and this book will ignite hope and faith in countless lives.

—Steve Backlund,
Co-Founder, Igniting Hope Ministries

PART 1

Dare to Dream Again

INTRODUCTION

You are Worthy of Your Dreams

> "Now to Him who is able to do immeasurably more than all we ask or imagine, according to His power that is at work within us."
>
> —Ephesians 3:20

If you're anything like I was years ago, you might have skipped over a book about dreaming with God. For most of my life, I was living in what I call *survival mode,* and dreaming didn't feel like an option. When my husband's affairs came out years ago, it was all I could do to keep my head above water. Have you ever been in a similar place of pain? I get it. I've experienced some of the most unimaginable heartache.

The thing is, God never intended for me to stay in survival mode, but for the longest time, dreaming with God was so hard for me to do. It was hard mostly because I felt so unworthy of big dreams. I lived most of my life without knowing Jesus. I wasn't saved until I was in my thirties. I like to say I was "late to the Jesus party." I had the hardest time imagining a life beyond survival, but after my salvation, God started speaking to me about how I was created for more. It wasn't through a dramatic encounter. It was just Him talking to my heart, and me knowing there must be so much more to my life than just surviving.

Slowly, I started talking to God about my dreams while journaling. I started dreaming about preaching the gospel, and encouraging women who had been through the same kind of pain I had been through. I used to think these thoughts were selfish. It wasn't until I went to ministry school with my husband that I started realizing it was God talking to me about my future. (Yes, our marriage was restored, which is a crazy, amazing testimony that I'll share later in this book.)

In ministry school, I began receiving prophetic words about teaching, preaching, and leading. My tiny world started opening up to the possibility that *maybe* I was created for more. I would say to myself, *"What if I was actually created to do big things?"* During ministry school, my heart was healing and opening up to the possibility that God wasn't mad at me for my past. Not only was He not mad at me, but *He actually loved me deeply* and had plans for me that went beyond what I could imagine.

The truth was, I felt unworthy to dream. I felt like a low-level Christian who had somehow snuck her way into this incredible ministry school (BSSM in Redding, California). I felt so unqualified, unworthy, and honestly, like a fake. I would think, "What if someone finds out about my past?" It wasn't that I was trying to hide my past—my husband

and I are really open about our story—but I was mostly worried that people would get to know the real me and decide they didn't like me. Ultimately, I was avoiding stepping into my dreams because I was afraid of being seen and known. There was a lie hiding in my heart: *"Will people like the real me?"*

Can you relate? I've discovered that *the enemy only comes after what's valuable.* My dreams were incredibly valuable to God, and so are yours. But we can only dream as far as we're willing to confront the enemy's lies. I had to face his lies, and believe me, there were plenty to choose from! Here are a few: *"I'm not qualified. What if I have nothing to say? Will anyone listen to me? I'm too old, so how can God possibly use me?"* I threw in the last one to make you laugh, but it's truly what I believed! We were surrounded by young, wild-eyed revivalists in ministry school, so I thought, *"What could God possibly do with my life?"*

But honestly, the real reason I wasn't stepping into my dreams was a long list of excuses and bad beliefs about myself—and ultimately, bad beliefs about God. The truth was, God wasn't mad at me, and He definitely wasn't putting limitations on me. While in ministry school, I started opening my heart to the possibility that God wanted me to dream with Him. I would imagine the future and say to myself, *"What if..."* Walking with God is a journey, but we're not on this journey just to survive, as I thought for so long. Our lives are a reflection of our Creator. He designed us with a big future in mind. I slowly realized that God wasn't limiting me, but *I was limiting God with my small thinking.*

I battled the lie that I needed to stay small and shrink back for most of my life, so this book is really about overcoming the fear of man and stepping out in ways I never thought I would. For most of my life, I felt unworthy to pursue my dreams and believe in what God had put inside me. Have you ever felt that way? Maybe you, too, have battled fear, intimidation, and unworthiness. But the truth is, we are worthy. We are anointed, gifted, powerful, brave, and smart—and the enemy knows it.

The enemy will try to convince you that your past defines your future, just as he did to me for so long. Ultimately, he wants us to feel unworthy to step into our dreams, as I did for years. Unworthiness will tell you that no matter what you do, you're never enough. It will say that people shouldn't invest in you because what you have to offer isn't special. It will claim your future is limited because of your past. It will whisper that God is somehow limiting what He can do in your life because something is wrong with you. Unworthiness will send the message that your past defines your future and that you're unworthy of stepping into your dreams.

For so long, I let my past dictate what I could and couldn't do. I wanted to write a book, but I had a list of reasons and excuses for why I couldn't: I had no college degree, I was previously divorced, I was a stay-at-home mom, and I had no writing experience. I thought my biggest skill set was "stay-at-home mom tennis." I felt unqualified, but as I started to unpack the feelings I was experiencing, I realized I was believing the lie that I was unworthy of stepping into my dreams.

I wrote this book to tell you that your past does not define your future, and there is literally nothing you can't do with God. There's a story inside you, a testimony, and ideas that the world needs. There's a business idea, a ministry idea—whatever your dream is, the world needs what only you can offer in the way only you can offer it. I believe that as you read this book, dreams will be reignited, and you might even start dreaming for the first time.

I used to struggle with preachers who said, "If you can do it without God, you're not dreaming big enough." The problem was, I knew they were right. I wanted to dream—really badly—but I didn't know how. That's what this book is about: my journey of hearing God for myself and realizing that He actually wants us to dream what I call *God-Sized Dreams.*

I never thought I'd write a book, lead a ministry, build a leadership academy, or become a pastor, licensed through my home church, Bethel. I never imagined I'd create courses, build a business from the ground up with my husband, or become the overseer of a large ministry. Years ago, these things would have sounded impossible to me. Throughout this book, I'll share how I overcame fear, intimidation, and the lie that I was unworthy to step into my dreams.

The dreams in our hearts are part of our *inheritance*, and each of us has an inheritance from God. I believe that as you read this book, the dreams in your heart will be reignited, and just like me, you'll take action steps to move toward your dreams. You were created for *great exploits* and with a significant purpose in mind. Let's go on a journey to unpack your God-Sized Dreams—not just to talk about them but to see your dreams, your inheritance, come to pass.

Melinda

CHAPTER 1

You Have an Inheritance

> "For we are God's handiwork, created in Christ Jesus to do good works, which God prepared in advance for us to do."
>
> —Ephesians 2:10

You have an inheritance—dreams to fulfill, a significant assignment, and great exploits to accomplish. The enemy wants us to feel like we have nothing significant to offer, but each of us has an inheritance from God—dreams that are unique to us. Throughout this book, I'll share several transformational keys and practical steps to access your dreams—your inheritance.

I've learned that so many people don't step into their dreams because, like I did for a long time, they believe they're unworthy and have nothing significant to offer. But I believe with all my heart that if God can transform me—a formerly unsaved, insecure, broken, divorced, stay-at-home mom without a college degree—to write a book, start and lead a ministry, become a pastor, create courses, build a leadership academy, and speak at conferences, then truly, anything is possible!

God has set every single person apart to accomplish great things. I love Daniel 11:32, which says, "…the people who know their God shall be strong, and carry out great exploits." There's no limit to what we can accomplish with God, but it wasn't until I started stepping out and doing what God called me to do that I realized what was inside me all along.

I had a significant dream one night about my inheritance—my dreams. In the dream, I was holding 14 rare gold coins, each worth one million dollars. My husband, Pieter, was beside me, looking at an old computer. I could see he was researching the 14 gold coins. Pieter said to me, "Melinda, the gold coins represent our inheritance." Suddenly, a woman appeared behind me. I knew she was there to steal my coins! I found myself being chased by her down a hill, but instead of running, I lay down and flew down the hill, safely reaching the bottom while holding the gold coins. Then I woke up.

After the dream, God spoke to my heart: "Melinda, the gold coins represent your inheritance. The woman is a spirit of fear and intimidation, trying to intimidate you out of stepping into your dreams." My gold coin dream revealed what was happening—the enemy was trying to intimidate me out of my inheritance, the dreams that were in my heart to accomplish.

One of those dreams was to write a book, but as I started writing, the enemy would tell me no one would read it. He'd say I should stop now because my book wasn't good. Has something similar ever happened to you? The enemy is a bully, but guess what? I listened to his lies and eventually stopped writing because I was so discouraged. I started believing I couldn't do it. Everything inside me screamed to give up and give in to the temptation to quit. But I also knew great leaders aren't born when things are easy; they're made when the pressure is on. Yes, the enemy wanted me to quit, and he hopes you'll quit too. But here's the thing: the only power the enemy has is the power we give him through our agreement. We will always reduce our lives down to our belief systems – which I will talk about more in another chapter.

Looking back at my life, I could see a cycle where I would start things and not complete them. I started college but didn't finish. I started a business but didn't finish. The reason I stopped short was fear—fear of failing and messing up. I also felt unworthy to accomplish great things because of my past. This book will not only help you identify your dreams and take steps forward but also help you overcome fear and intimidation so you can not only start your dreams but complete them. The enemy wants us to quit because there is so much *power in completion.*

I received a prophetic word as I was preparing to write my second book. The person said to me, "Melinda, if you don't quit, you win!" The enemy wants us to quit, stop, and settle for less than what God has for us. He'll work hard to ensure you don't complete the dreams in your heart because of the many people your dreams will impact. But I also know that as you move forward with action steps of faith, like I did, you'll see your dreams unfold right before your eyes.

I had dreams in my heart about teaching and writing, but I never thought they'd actually happen. I was so afraid to step out and do what God called me to do because I believed the lie that I was unworthy and had nothing significant to offer. But I've realized that if we don't step out and "do it afraid," we'll never discover what God has placed inside us. We can't wait to feel different; we have to do something different and believe something different.

Our Dreams Are Us and For Others

The truth is, someone out there is waiting for us to step into our dreams. Our dreams aren't just for ourselves; they're for others. I was terrified to speak at the first marriage conference with my husband. I had never done anything like that before, and it involved one of my biggest fears—public speaking. But something incredible happened after I stepped out and did it afraid. People wrote to us and shared how much hope the conference gave them for their marriage.

Just the other day, my husband and I were at an event, and a couple approached us. They told us how impactful the marriage event was for their marriage. They said it was a huge catalyst for them to stay in their marriage and believe it could be better than ever. These testimonies show that what we carry inside us is needed by others. Our breakthrough isn't just for us; it's for many. My gold coin dream revealed that I could either bury my talents—my dreams, gifts, calling, and inheritance—or step out and say no to fear and intimidation.

I love the story of Elijah. He accomplished great things with the Lord and lived an incredibly supernatural life. He killed the false prophets of Baal, raised the dead, and performed other miracles. Yet, one woman, Jezebel, threatened to kill him, and he ran for his life and hid in a cave (1 Kings 19)! That's how convincing fear and intimidation can be. They try to make us run from our calling, hide in a cave, and bury our talents.

What we allow to speak to us will determine where we're going. There is power in our agreement. For most of my life, I agreed with the lie that I was unworthy and unqualified. I was too intimidated to try anything new, so I buried my talents. However, when I finally started intentionally stepping out and doing what I was called to do, everything changed.

Deeply Loved by God

Before we go any further, I also want to stop and say, although our dreams are for others, they are also for us. Anyone who has a child knows that you would do absolutely anything for that child. If our child's dream is to get a trampoline, a doll, or a race car set for Christmas, we want to give it to them! It's like we are hard-wired to want to give our kids *the best* of everything. God is the same way with us! His desire is to give His kids the best of everything! Religion has taught us that God is withholding from us or that God is somehow mad at us, but that's simply not the truth. Nahum 1:7 says, "God is good" and 1 John 4:8 says, "God is love." Goodness, love, and kindness are God's nature, and He can never contradict who He is.

We are deeply loved children, and God designed us with a great purpose in mind. God said to the prophet Jeremiah, "Before I formed you in the womb I knew you, before you were born I set you apart; I appointed you as a prophet to the nations." Jeremiah 1:15 NIV. I love that God spoke identity to Jeremiah before he sent him out to do great exploits. Before he stepped into his assignment and calling as a prophet, God wanted Jeremiah to know that he was deeply loved and chosen by God.

Psalm 139 says God formed us in our mother's womb. The NIV version says "You covered me in my mother's womb." We are all deeply loved, covered, and known by God. Yes, our calling is for others, but we can dream big because we have *a really good Dad,* who loves us deeply and wants to see us step into the abundant life Jesus came to give to us (John 10:10). Yes, we will accomplish great things for the Lord, but everything is done in relationship with Him. God formed us in our mother's womb. Before we step out, it's important to know first that we are loved for *who* we are, and not *what* we do.

Steps to Start Dreaming Again

Throughout this book, I share with you the 6-steps to Dare to Dream Again. This book will also give you practical tools and steps to overcome fear and intimidation and to walk boldly into your God-Sized Dreams. You were created for *great exploits!* You were created to make a significant impact in the lives of others. As you read these pages, you'll receive deeper revelation of the dreams in your heart and who your dreams will impact. Your dreams are your inheritance, and they're not just for you—they're for many!

Step 1: Dare to Dream Again

Maybe you're like me years ago and you feel like you don't know how to dream. Or maybe you're in a season of feeling like you're in survival mode. I get it. I have been there. But, I've discovered that there is power in agreement, so the first step in starting to dream again is to simply acknowledge that you are loved, and you were created to make an impact. It's ok if you don't see the whole thing right now. You can start by saying, "I am going to start dreaming again." That's really the first step.

Next is to agree that you were created to make an impact in this world. If you don't feel that way right now, it's ok. Part of the process is to trust that God will show you what you were created to do. If you feel stuck at the idea of starting to dream like I did for a long time, great questions to ask yourself are these: Who do I have compassion for? Who do I want to help? What is my testimony? What have I overcome that others need? Who do I have a heart to help?

Step 2: Get a Vision for Your Dream

The second step to discovering your dreams is to get a clear vision for your dreams. Habakkuk 2:2 says, "Write the vision; make it plain on tablets..." Have you ever written down your goals in a journal, only to forget them days later? I've done that many times! Keeping the vision in front of you helps to remember your "why"—why you're getting up at 5 a.m. to write each morning or why you're taking that class or meeting with that person. Without a prophetic vision, the people perish. We need a clear vision to keep going.

During step two, we will use our Godly imaginations by asking great questions like: What will my dream look like? What will it feel like to see it unfold? Example: If your dream is to write a book you can ask: What does it look like to see myself holding the book? Who is reading the book? What color is the book? How many chapters does the book have? How does the cover feel? We will use our Godly imaginations to see the vision in front of us and keep it in front of us.

We will also ask ourselves additional questions like: What lies has the enemy been telling me about my dreams? What is the truth about my dreams? We will break down the lies, vows (internal agreements), and get the truth, so that we can step into our dreams. The truth makes us free and the truth frees us to dream big with God (see Romans 12:2). Lies can sometimes be subtle and can have a huge impact on our calling. Identifying lies and replacing those lies with truth is a huge key to stepping into our dreams.

Step 3: See Who Your Dreams will Impact

The next step is to see a picture of who our dreams will impact. Our dreams are not for just ourselves, they are for others! Who needs my dream to come to pass? Who needs that book I am going to write? Who will be impacted by my dream coming to pass?

Maybe you feel called to help the homeschool community or maybe you feel called to women in the entrepreneur and business sphere. What does it look like when you have the opportunity to speak to those women individually or in a group setting? In what ways have you impacted women's lives? We will also ask ourselves the hard questions like, what will happen if we say no to the dream? Or what lies has the enemy been telling me about who my dreams will impact? What is the truth?

Keeping a clear picture of who our dreams will reach is a key to stepping into them. Our dreams aren't just for us; they're for others! I believe thousands of marriages will be healed and restored because of my marriage restoration testimony. I believe my books will reach thousands and thousands of women. Keeping the "who" in front of you will keep us motivated to keep going. We step into our dreams so lives will be transformed, people will be healed and delivered, and others can step into their dreams too.

Step 4: Forgive, Release, and Bless

Forgiveness is one of the greatest gifts from Jesus needed to go after our God-sized dreams. I have personally experienced pain, heartache, and betrayal at the deepest level when my husband's affairs came out. I was devastated and could have easily kept my heart hardened towards my husband. But I have discovered that unforgiveness is one of the biggest "destiny blockers" I've ever seen. I call unforgiveness and bitterness (bitterness is prolonged unforgiveness) a "destiny destroyer". The enemy hopes we will "take the bait" and live offended so that we won't be able to step into our dreams, but I have learned that forgiveness fully releases us and allows us to step into the dreams God has placed in our hearts.

Joseph's life is a powerful example of what God can do with someone who is willing to forgive and bless his enemies. Joseph was sold into slavery by his own brothers, and they were reunited years later. Joseph's intentional forgiveness of his brothers, allowed him to rule and reign as second in command to all of Egypt. It says in Genesis 50 that Joseph spoke kindly to his brothers and took care of them and their children. Joseph had the heart of a leader who could be trusted to lead people. We will go through the steps of forgiveness in this book, so that you can move forward into your destiny to rule and reign, just like Joseph!

Step 5: Plan, Action, and Movement

The next step is the practical side of dreaming. Once we have a vision, we need a plan to move forward. We can have a vision, and still get nothing done. Example: Let's say your goal is to write a book. Questions to ask yourself are: How many chapters will I need to complete each month in order for my book to be edited and published in six months? How much time will I need to set aside each day to write? Who will edit the book? Will you self-publish? When is my own deadline? Let's say your goal is to start a business. What are the first things you will need to get started in order to launch the business: (location, website, social media page, budget, revenue goal, payment processing system, etc.).

Taking steps forward each day, regardless of how we feel, is a huge key to stewarding our dreams. I used to wait to feel anointed to write, and wouldn't you know, I hardly wrote anything on most days, because I was waiting for a feeling! A huge key to my breakthrough was overcoming the lie that I had to feel anointed for my writing to be anointed. Waiting for our feelings to line up in order to move forward will keep us from accomplishing our dreams.

I know this well from personal experience because when I actually started to write consistently, regardless of how I was feeling, I found joy in the process. My confidence to write actually grew as I moved forward. I like to say the anointing is for action! We all have a unique anointing to do what you are called to do (1 John 2:20 & 27). The anointing is with you and is the person of the Holy Spirit upon your life to help you do what God has called you to do. The Holy Spirit doesn't come and go. Jesus said I will be with you always (Matthew 28:20). This means, the person of the Holy Spirit is in us and with us always, regardless of how we feel.

Throughout this book, we will make action steps to move forward and step into our dreams. We won't see changes by sitting still. As I took steps forward to write my book, I discovered that action steps were a huge key to seeing my dreams unfold right before my eyes. That book won't write itself, so we must intentionally take action steps of faith each day if we want to see our dreams come to pass. Whatever God has called you to do, He has anointed you to do. God blesses what we prepare for.

Step 6: Completion of the Dream!

The final step is to complete your dream, and see it come to pass. Too many people quit and never complete what they have started. This was me for a long time, but I have discovered there is power in completion. The enemy really hopes you will give up because there is tremendous power in completion. Galatians 6:9 promises that we will reap a harvest if we do not give up.

In conclusion, this book will give you practical tools and steps to overcome fear and intimidation and to walk boldly into your God-Sized Dreams. You were created for *great exploits!* You were created to make a significant impact in the lives of others. As you read these pages, you'll receive deeper revelation of the dreams in your heart and who your dreams will impact. Your dreams are your inheritance, and they're not just for you—they're for many!

Prophetic Word

You are someone who Dares to Dream Again, and you dream BIG! You are anointed to teach people how to dream with God, and that dreaming with God means dreaming with *no limits!* God has placed dreams in your heart, and He will guide you to fulfill them. You are called to greatness. God has destined you for a purpose that will impact nations, and He has equipped you now for every step. "For we are His workmanship, created in Christ Jesus for good works, which God prepared beforehand that we should walk in them." (Ephesians 2:10)

Truth Declarations

- God is able to do exceedingly, abundantly above all I ask or imagine. (Ephesians 3:20)
- God's promises are my inheritance. (Hebrews 6:17)
- God is watching over His Word to perform it in my life. (Jeremiah 1:12)

- I receive every promise by faith. (Hebrews 11:1)
- All things work together for my good. (Romans 8:28)

CHAPTER 2

Stepping Into Your God-Sized D.R.E.A.M.S

The following are *five key mindsets* that have been a tremendous help to me as I have stepped into my dreams. I love acronyms, so I created one from one of my favorite words: D.R.E.A.M.S.

- **D – Destined for Impact** – I was created to have a big impact.
- **R – Reimagine My Dreams** – I imagine my dreams with limitless thinking and I dream BIG.
- **E – Enlarge My Vision** – I constantly enlarge the vision of my dreams.
- **A – Action Steps Forward** – I take action steps forward into my dreams.
- **M – Movement and Momentum** – I am creating movement and momentum.
- **S – Stay away from the Dream Pessimists** – I surround myself with dream optimests.

D – Destined for Impact

Declaration: I was created to have a significant impact!

"No one can say it like you!"

—Steve Backlund

I was in a meeting with my boss, Steve Backlund, discussing the fears and insecurities I had about stepping out and publishing my first book—there were many, by the way! Steve said to me, "Melinda, no one can say it like you!" Steve is more than my boss; he is an exceptional leader who builds big people and sees them step into their dreams. Great leaders know they have an assignment, and that assignment isn't just for them. Great leaders know their assignment is to help others step into their dreams too.

The first mindset to have as you start dreaming again is to realize that absolutely *no one can say it like you or do it like you.* You have a unique anointing and calling that no one else has. Other people need what only you can offer to the world.

For so long, it was hard for me to believe I had something that others needed, but I had a dream one night where I was running a marathon on Highway 5 in California, and I was holding a baton. Many other women were running behind me. The women would run past me, and I would pass the batons to them. The women would run ahead and pass the batons to those running beside them. I realized my dreams were not just for me, they were so that I could pass my baton to others. My dreams were so that others could step into their dreams too. I needed to push past any guilt or feelings of being unworthy, unqualified, or selfish for wanting to step into my dreams. I love the parable of the man who buried his talent in Matthew 25. In this parable, Jesus was impressed with the servants who stewarded their talents well. In order to step into our dreams, we must stop feeling guilty for wanting to dream big and increase our talents.

For most of my life, I buried my gifts and talents because I felt unworthy, but it was also out of a fear of messing up. I was just like the servant who buried his one talent. I was so afraid of doing the right thing, that I actually did nothing! Jesus did not die so we could be unproductive, unfulfilled, and miserable Christians. Jesus died so we could have life, and life abundantly (John 10:10). The word "abundant" means "excessive and overflowing." Romans 5:17 says we will "reign in life through Jesus Christ." People who rule and reign are those living fully alive, having fully stepped into what God has called them to do.

I also realized I had to give myself permission to dream about the impact my dreams would make. Like I mentioned before, for the longest time, I was stuck in what I call "survival mode." I was just trying to survive—forget about dreaming! During this season, my sister was diagnosed with a brain tumor and went through multiple surgeries. My husband's affairs came to light. My dad was diagnosed with cancer and moved in with us—and the long list of trials went on.

I truly thought "survival mode" was as good as it gets! I never thought I would write a book because all I could focus on was just getting through each day, but I had a dream in my heart to write. However, for so long, I wouldn't allow myself to dream because in addition to feeling unworthy, I was afraid of being disappointed if the dream didn't happen. Dreams require risk. Risk means we might dream only to be disappointed. But I've also learned the risk far outweighs the cost of not dreaming. We actually risk not stepping into what we were created to do if we don't step out and try.

R - Reimagine My Dreams

Declaration: I imagine my dreams as BIG!

My childhood was filled with wonderful moments, but also with pain, frustration, and disappointment. I was exhausted when I gave my life back to the Lord as a thirty-something year-old woman. God began to speak to me while I was in ministry school about my future. He said staying in "survival mode" was a mindset, and I could choose what to believe about my past, present, and future. God was not holding me back from my dreams, *but my perspective and beliefs about my past were limiting God.* I was avoiding taking action steps forward because of the lies I believed and the conclusions I had made.

We tell ourselves stories all the time through our imaginations, and sometimes those stories lead to excuses for why we can't do what we're called to do. For example, I told myself that because of my history of failed public speaking, I wasn't meant to speak. My conclusions created excuses that made me feel safe. I mentioned earlier that risk involves the possibility of disappointment, so our brains create reasons why we can't do what we're called to do.

For me, public speaking was *painful*. The problem was, I was allowing my imagination to create conclusions based on my past, which limited my destiny. The main point of reimagining is to learn how to rewrite our story—past, present, and future—so we can run after our dreams. Proverbs 23:7 tells us, "As a man thinks in his heart, so is he." If a person's thoughts shape their destiny, we must be intentional about what we think and the conclusions we make about our past, present, and future.

We can reimagine a new past, present, and future and tell our brains a new story to shape our destiny. The enemy targets our thoughts and imaginations because he knows if he can limit our thinking, or get us to believe lies based on conclusions, he can significantly limit our power, effectiveness, and destiny. For a long time, I was limited in what I could do because of what I believed. The conclusions I made, and the stories I told myself, kept me bound to the narratives I created. But my biggest transformation came when I decided to reimagine what my life could look like.

Remember, I used to imagine myself failing every time I spoke in front of a group. And wouldn't you know, that's exactly what happened when I got up to speak—*it was painful!* The difficulty came because I imagined failing instead of succeeding. I was allowing the narrative of my past to determine my future. It wasn't until I started telling myself a new story and imagining myself successfully speaking that things changed.

Practically, this looked like spending time with God and meditating on the truth. I reimagined the past event and created a new narrative in my mind about what the future would look like. Much to my shock, imagining something different actually worked! I shifted what I was imagining to the point that I began to enjoy public speaking, which I previously thought was impossible. I went from dreading speaking to wanting to teach. We will break down more steps in this book to reminagin our future using our Godly imaginations.

E - Enlarge My Vision

Declaration: I constantly enlarge my vision of my dreams!

When I set out to write my first book, I had no clear vision of why the book was being written or who it would impact. Then, as I was writing, I heard Terri Savelle Foy say, "You need a vision for your dream." Having a vision is biblical. Jesus made a declaration about His dreams when He declared Isaiah 61 over Himself, before He had performed any miracles, He had a clear vision of where He was going, what He would be doing, and who He would impact. Proverbs 29:18 says, "Where there is no prophetic vision, the people perish." We need a clear vision of our dreams, future, and goals to keep going. Without a clear vision of who we will impact, we lose momentum and forget why we're doing what we're doing.

For example, when I started my second book—the one you're reading now—I sat down and asked God for a vision for the book. I wanted to see why God needed me to write it. The Holy Spirit showed me many women stepping into their dreams as a result of my book. He showed me mindsets from the past being ripped out of people and He showed me a picture of people being delivered from self-limiting mindsets. He told me dreams would be discovered and fulfilled as a result of my book. Keeping the mindset that I was created to have a significant impact on other people was a huge key for me to stay motivated and keep going. Throughout this book, we will get a clear vision for who your dreams will impact, so that you can enlarge your vision, and can keep the vision in front of you.

A - Action Steps Forward

Declaration: I take steps forward into my dreams!

A good place to start taking steps forward is to a dream journal or vision board where you can clearly see your dreams and goals. I got this idea from Terri Savelle Foy, "The Dream Cheerleader." I started writing down my prophetic words and the dreams God put in my heart. I would first sit quietly with the Lord and write down what He was saying about my life. I started making a journal by adding photos and images I printed from the internet that matched what God showed me. I started reading my dreams every day, praying over my dreams, and declaring them out loud.

Before I knew about the concept of a "dream journal" I would write down a declaration of my daughter Kaitlyn's salvation. I would sit with God and imagine her salvation moment happening. Then I would thank God in advance for her salvation. I was using the concept of using my sanctified imagination to visualize and partner with what God wanted to do, without realizing it was a huge key to seeing my dreams come to pass. And guess what? My daughter, Kaitlyn, was saved, and she just graduated from her third and final year of ministry school!

We will dive into the steps to create a dream journal or dream board in the last part of this book. This step is so important because a dream journal or vision board will help you keep the dream you're believing in clearly in front of you, so that when you take action steps forward you will remember why we are doing what we are doing.

M – Movement and Momentum

Declaration: I am creating movement and momentum!

One thing I've learned is we'll never fully feel alive until we start moving forward in what we're called to do. I sat down to write my first book—feeling completely unqualified—and the enemy whispered, *"You're not an author. This book will never sell. You should just quit."* The enemy is a liar, but the way to fight back is to move forward.

For example, when I started writing my book and felt the enemy's lies, I would stop writing and declare, "I am an author, and my books sell thousands of copies." It was a battle for sure, but I've realized we don't get unstuck by sitting still. We have to move to see transformation. I like to say about stepping into our dreams: "No one grows successful sitting still; we grow as we go."

Of course, the enemy will try to lie and tell you that you have nothing significant to say or offer. He's just worried you'll figure out how powerful you are. I had prophetic words that I would write books, preach, and teach. I made it onto Steve Backlund's team during my third year of ministry school. I literally said to myself, "I'll just be the one who doesn't speak. I'll sit on the sidelines." But Steve and his wife, Wendy, incredible empowering leaders, said, "Melinda, we see destiny in you! You are meant to speak."

Steve and Wendy put their belief in me into practice by giving me opportunities to speak. I encountered many lies during this season, but God was calling me to believe in myself and my dreams. Transformation didn't happen right away, but as I intentionally stepped out and tried, I started believing I had something significant to offer. The same is true for you. You are anointed, and the enemy knows it. What you have to offer the world is unique and powerful.

Nehemiah was also taunted by the enemy for wanting to step into his dream of rebuilding the walls of Jerusalem. Nehemiah's response to the enemy's taunting is inspirational: "So I sent messengers to them, saying, 'I am doing a great work, so that I cannot come down. Why should the work cease while I leave it and go down to you?'" (Nehemiah 6:3). Nehemiah understood his role for God was so significant that he couldn't stop to consider what the enemy was saying.

Just like Nehemiah, the enemy will always be ready to taunt us when we're doing a great work for the Lord. He'll use people to discourage us, distract us, and get our eyes off God's promises and the dreams He's put in our hearts. *He'll especially get us to focus on what's not happening.* But I've discovered his lies are an illusion based on perceived conclusions. Just like Nehimiah, we gain momentum as we go and take action steps forward.

I sometimes think of how many things are not built in the Kingdom of God because people stop taking action when faced when opposition is faced:

"I was going to write that book, but the enemy told me it wouldn't be good…"
"I was going to run that marathon, but I faced opposition…"
"I was going to start that business, but I was rejected by investors…"
"I was going to … but…"

S - Stay Away from Dream Pessimists

Declaration: I surround myself with dream optimests.

The final mindset to have as we step into our dreams is to give ourselves permission to stay away from "dream pessimists." Not everyone will understand you or what you're called to do, and that's ok. Dream pessimists are people who don't see you for your prophetic potential. The goal of the prophetic is to see people according to their future, not their past or present. One key is to surround yourself with people who speak life and encouragement into your destiny, not "destiny pessimists" who give you reasons why you shouldn't dream. Often, "destiny pessimists" list reasons you shouldn't pursue your dreams because they need to validate why they stopped short of stepping into their own.

My husband, Pieter, met with a physician who was a believer. The doctor told him his idea to launch a medical device company based on an invention would never work and would likely fail. We can love others and be kind to them but also realize the enemy may use certain people to discourage us and get us to quit. Stay away from these people and avoid letting them speak into your life. My husband was also turned down by multiple investors who said his idea would never work. Today, our company is successful, thriving, and growing each day.

The same week we launched our ministry, someone emailed us, saying it wasn't biblical to offer inner healing and deliverance to the church. I wanted to write back and defend what we were called to do, but the Holy Spirit said to me, "Melinda, forgive the person, bless them, and move on." The Lord reminded me that my battle was not with flesh and blood. The person who wrote to us was not the enemy. I could have let that person stop us from starting our ministry, or I could forgive, bless, and move on. Not everyone will be excited about what you're doing, and that's okay.

Prophetic Word

Absolutely *no one can say it like you or do it like you.* You have a unique anointing and calling that no one else has. There is not a single person in the world with your exact assignment. Just like the Apostles you are *anointed for impact.* Your unique gifts will bring heaven to earth in ways only you can. "The Spirit of the Lord is upon me, because He has anointed me to preach good tidings to the poor." (Isaiah 61:1)

Faith Declarations

- I receive every promise by faith. (Hebrews 11:1)
- I am rooted and grounded in God's promises.
- I live in expectation of God's goodness.
- I stand firm in God's unshakeable Kingdom. (Hebrews 12:28)
- I am an heir to the promises of Abraham. (Galatians 3:29)

CHAPTER 3

Speak Life Over Your Dreams

"The words we speak today create the reality we will live in tomorrow."

—Melinda Lagaay

My husband competed in the Olympics for field hockey. He told me one of the main ways Olympic athletes mentally prepare is through imagination. They would visualize the game before setting foot on the field. Pieter said he and his teammates imagined every shot, score, play, and outcome—every victory was envisioned before it happened. Not only that, they would declare the outcome as though it had already occurred.

Today, it's common for athletes to practice seeing the victory before it happens. Why do professional teams invest so much time and energy in this? They understand a biblical concept from Proverbs 29:18, which says, "Where there is no prophetic vision, the people perish." We need a vision for our lives, and we must see it before it happens. Radically successful people don't waste time thinking about or speaking unproductive things. To change our lives, we must first imagine something different and then speak something different.

The Blue Angels

A team of pilots known worldwide as the Blue Angels flies at incredible speeds of 120 to 700 mph. They are among the top-ranking pilots in the world. Before every flight, the Blue Angels do something remarkable: they conduct an intensive pre-flight briefing, closing their eyes and mentally flying the entire routine. They practice every turn, formation shift, and even hear the radio calls.

They succeed in the air because they've flown the routine in their minds first. What we focus on, we produce. What we imagine becomes our reality. Steve Backlund says, "There is no limit to how much we can renew our minds, so there is no limit to how much we can be transformed." His wife, Wendy, an international speaker and author, says, "The imagination is the womb of faith." What we imagine and focus on, we will eventually give birth to. We must ask ourselves, are we imagining ourselves successful, or are we imagining ourselves according to our past failures? The next section contains several practical keys to start speaking life over our dreams and imagining a new future with God.

Key 1 - Reimagine Your Past, Present, and Future

Our experiences are real, but they, whether good or bad, cause us to form conclusions based on how we process them. In my case, I concluded I could not or should not speak publicly. I reduced my life to the level of my belief system, limiting what I could do. Our imaginations are powerful but not always truthful. For the longest time, I imagined the future through the lens of my past failures.

I would tell myself a story about my failure repeatedly until I believed it. That story had conclusions attached: "I am a failure. I can't measure up. I can't be a public speaker." Inner healing ministry calls these conclusions "lies" and encourages replacing them with truth. I've taught this technique to others, but through research and experience, I've learned we must go beyond replacing lies. We must tell ourselves a new story to create new conclusions, because our conclusions become belief systems, and our belief systems shape our reality. We live according to the level of our belief systems.

The good news is God wired our brains with the incredible ability to be transformed, meaning we can choose what we believe and be transformed as a result. Romans 12:2 says, "Be transformed by the renewing of your mind." The brain's job is to process information and form conclusions to keep us safe. Neuroscientists say our brains make sense of our lives. Essentially, our brains create stories based on conclusions, which aren't always facts. Thankfully, God designed us with the ability to be transformed by renewing our minds.

Scientists call this ability neuroplasticity. Dr. Caroline Leaf, a cognitive neuroscientist and Christian author, defines neuroplasticity as the brain's God-designed ability to change, rewire, and heal through the choices we make in our thinking. She emphasizes that our thoughts actively shape our brain's structure.

For example, whenever someone mentioned public speaking, I would unintentionally rehearse my high school experience, and feelings of shame, failure, and inadequacy would surface. The story I told myself was that I could not speak publicly. My husband and I attended ministry school together, and in our third year, you applied to various mentorship programs. I applied to join Steve Backlund's team, along with my husband. I knew the team always had dynamic public speakers, but I thought, "I'll just be in the background. I don't want a microphone." Truthfully, I was hiding from my calling, like Gideon in the winepress.

The Backlund team consisted of seven men and me—a woman. I was terrified, but something told me I was supposed to be there. Steve and Wendy Backlund, mind renewal experts, helped me realize the number of lies I believed about myself. I had no idea my thoughts were common and that many people struggled similarly.

While on the team, I received prophetic words that I would write books and speak to thousands of women. Writing and public speaking were the two areas I felt most unqualified for. I had concluded that because of a bad public speaking experience years ago, I wasn't meant to speak. Conclusions can include: "Your past defines you. You'll never succeed. You're not worthy. You should be embarrassed about your past." I know personally that shame loves to partner with a victim spirit, guilt, and self-condemnation.

I learned to reduce my life to my belief system to avoid discomfort. We always reduce our lives to the level of truth or lies we believe, unintentionally self-sabotaging to match our belief systems—the conclusions we've made. The more freedom I have in my mindsets, the freer I am to dream, create, and build with God. I used to think dreaming was impossible. I struggled to see past my failures and perceived shortcomings, but God started showing me I was limiting what He could do through me because of my conclusions. He also told me I needed to start declaring something different to see change, which brings me to my next point: speak life over your dreams.

Key 2 – Speak Life Over Our Dreams

I heard a preacher say there's a country in Africa whose king wears a veil over his mouth because every word he speaks could become law. His words are powerful enough to change a nation! Similarly, our words hold tremendous power. In this chapter, I'll discuss the power of our words, because they can either launch us into our dreams and destiny or hold us back. Proverbs 18:21 says, "Death and life are in the power of the tongue, and those who love it will eat its fruit." I like to say, "The words we speak today create the reality we will live in tomorrow."

Have you heard of Dr. Emoto? He's a Japanese scientist who aimed to prove our words hold power. Dr. Emoto conducted an experiment with three jars of water and rice. He spoke to the first jar, saying "thank you," to the second, "you're an idiot," and ignored the third. After 30 days, the rice that was told "you're an idiot" turned black, the ignored rice rotted, and the "thanked" rice fermented into a pleasant aroma.

God started speaking to me about the words I was declaring over my life. For the longest time, I was cursing myself while expecting God to bless me. I'd say things like, "That's just the way it is," "I'm exhausted and never have energy," "We never have enough money," or "I'll never lose weight." My friend Connie Jones, a John Maxwell Certified Coach and Significant Leader at Igniting Hope, suggests adding this to your words to test if you should speak them: "And that's just the way I like it."

- "I'm exhausted all the time—and that's just the way I like it."
- "I never have enough money to pay the bills—and that's just the way I like it."
- "My marriage will never change—and that's just the way I like it."
- "My kids don't respect me—and that's just the way I like it."
- "My job is killing me—and that's just the way I like it."
- "I'll never lose weight—and that's just the way I like it."

I jokingly say, "Forget the devil—I was doing his job by cursing myself for years. I'm surprised he didn't send me a thank-you card!" It's funny to say aloud, but how often have we spoken against God's promises and expected blessings? I've done it many times! The good news is, you can start speaking life today, but we must speak something different to see something different manifest.

Key 3 - Make Decrees Over Your Dreams

Job 22:28 (NASB) says, "You will also decree a thing, and it will be established for you; and light will shine on your ways." A decree is a "royal proclamation"—we are kings and priests of our God, so every word we speak, good or bad, sets things in motion. Like the African king whose words become law, our words give the enemy a legal right to harass us or send angels on assignment to accomplish God's plans (Matthew 12:36).

During a chaotic season when my marriage was falling apart, my daughter was struggling with friendships, our finances were a mess, my father was dying, and everything in our home was breaking, I had a pity party. While grumbling one day, the Lord said, "Melinda, you can partner with what you see in the natural realm, or you can speak and declare the opposite."

Jesus said it's not what enters our mouth that defiles us, but what comes out (Matthew 15:11). This wasn't meant to make us fear our words but to show their tremendous power. Creating with our words is a privilege. We can speak life everywhere and prophecy truth into every situation. There is power in our words to build up our future or destroy it.

Key 4 - Speak to Your Dreams

> "95% of our emotions are determined by the way you talk to yourself."
>
> —Brian Tracy

Remember how I avoided public speaking my entire life because I told myself I wasn't meant to speak? I had a terrible experience in high school where I gave a speech and I awkwardly fumbled my words, finished a 10-minute speech in two minutes (all while sweating profusely), and sat back down. I was completely embarrassed. I remember that moment like it was yesterday, filled with shame, fear, and embarrassment. After that speech, I said to myself, "I will never speak in public again." God wasn't limiting my destiny; my self-talk was limiting my destiny. I was terrified of speaking in public, even though deep down, I knew I was called to do it.

What really transformed my life was realizing I was limiting what God could do through me because of how I was talking to myself. I had to intentionally challenge every thought that wasn't in line with what God was saying about me and then declare the truth out loud.

Satan hopes we won't grasp how powerful our words are. He knows that if you understand your authority to declare God's Word, it's game over for him! He can only work where we give him permission. For something to manifest in the natural realm, a believer must take authority, pray, and say something! Job 22:28 (NASB) says, "You will also declare a thing, and it will be established for you; so light will shine on your ways." God gave me and you authority, dominion, and permission to rule as ambassadors of Christ, but nothing happens until we rise up and say something.

When my husband's affairs came to light, Pieter had his own encounter with God and gave his life to Jesus, all while I had my own encounter where I heard the audible voice of God say to me "I am going to restore your marriage". Though that was a deeply encouraging thing to hear at that moment, I had to battle so many doubts and lies from the enemy about our marriage. One day, while driving to the store, I had this thought: "Did God really say He was going to restore my marriage?" As soon as the thought came, the Holy Spirit said, "Melinda, replace the lie with the truth!" I now know that God was training me to be aware that not all thoughts were mine. I now know *any thought* leading me to hopelessness is from the enemy.

In that moment in the car, I knew I had to choose what I was going to believe about my future and about my marriage, so I laughed out loud and boldly declared, "My marriage is restored in Jesus' name! Pieter and I have an amazing marriage!" Then I turned the worship music up and started praising God for restoring my marriage as I drove down the road.

Terri Savelle Foy says, "There is a miracle in your mouth." And I like to say, "Nothing happens until someone says something." We have the power to declare the Word of God and see things manifest in our lives (Romans 4:17, Job 22:28). The enemy wants us to focus on what's not happening, and speak out his lies, but as we keep our eyes on what God has said, doubt will dissipate.

Key 5 - Overcome Gossip and Word Curses

Since we're discussing the power of our words, I want to address overcoming gossip. Though not the most heartwarming topic, it's important because many relationships are ruined by harmful or careless words. Our words hold power. Recall Dr. Emoto's rice experiment: the rice that was told "you're an idiot" *rotted*. This is a powerful visual of the impact our words can have on other people's lives.

Once I realized my words' power, I had to start examining my conversations. Much of what I and others called "processing" was actually gossip in disguise. I've gossiped under the guise of "processing," but God convicted me that I was putting a pretty name on something demonic. We're called to love our brothers and sisters in Christ and pray for our enemies. I've been hurt by others' words, and I'm sure you have too. Our words either send arrows of destruction or arrows of protection and life.

One of my core values not is a "no gossip" rule. I want to be known as someone who only sees the gold in others and speaks that gold out. If I have a problem with someone, I need to go directly to the person instead of "processing" my pain with others. I understand we can't always restore broken relationships, and we must have boundaries, but we can control what we say about those people. The power is really in our hands to speak life or death over our relationships.

In conclusion, we must realize that our words are powerful, and God expects us to believe His Word will work and accomplish something when we send it out. Isaiah 55:11 says, "So will My word be which goes out of My mouth; it will not return to Me empty, without accomplishing what I desire, and without succeeding in the purpose for which I sent it." God's Word achieves what it's sent to do! The question is, what are we sending out? What are we speaking out over our circumstances, our marriages, our jobs, our ministries, our friends, our churches, and our children?

We must realize how powerful and responsible we are for our words. We can't speak chaos and expect blessings. Jesus said we'll account for every idle word. Matthew 12:36 (AMPC) says, "But I tell you, on the day of judgment men will have to give account for every idle (inoperative, non-working) word they speak."

Have you been around someone who is destructive with their words? It's hard to be around them because they release so much negativity into the atmosphere. Conversely, someone who speaks life draws us in. Jesus spoke life, and crowds were drawn to Him. I want to be known for speaking life everywhere I go, and I know you do too!

Prophetic Word

Your words are a fountain of life, shaping your future! As you declare God's promises, you're aligning with His plans for you. Your voice is breaking chains and sparking hope in others. Speak boldly, for your words carry His power (Proverbs 18:21). Your words create life. As you declare God's truth, you are calling forth what does not yet exist. "[God] calls those things which do not exist as though they did." (Romans 4:17)

Truth Declarations

- I walk by faith, not by sight. (2 Corinthians 5:7)
- God's Word never returns void. (Isaiah 55:11)
- I will not waver in unbelief but will grow strong in faith. (Romans 4:20-21)
- I walk by faith, not by sight. (2 Corinthians 5:7)
- My words are powerful, so I choose to speak life today!

CHAPTER 4

Your Generational Inheritance

"We can view our past and family history through the lens of failure or through the lens of God's restoration and redemption."

—Melinda Lagaay

After my gold coin dream in Chapter 1, God asked me to start viewing my generational line through the lens of redemption and restoration. *God's plan is always to redeem and restore the generations.* In my dream, I held 14 gold coins, each representing one million dollars. As I prayed and researched, I discovered the number 14 symbolizes generational blessings.

> "So all the generations from Abraham to David are fourteen generations, from David until the captivity in Babylon are fourteen generations, and from the captivity in Babylon until the Christ are fourteen generations."
>
> —Matthew 1:17

Even the Hebrew numerical value of the word "gold" is 14. In Exodus 12:6–36, God kept His 400+ year promise to bring Israel out of slavery—on the 14th day of the month. The number 14 represents God moving on behalf of His people to fulfill His promises (Troy Brewer, *Numbers that Preach*). The Lord said to me, "Melinda, the gold coins represent your dreams, but they also represent the generational blessings in your family line."

Every family line has blessings and an inheritance—gifts, dreams, talents, and abilities. For example, my mother is an incredible leader, and for a season, she was a leader on the executive team for an international airline, traveling worldwide for her job. She possessed remarkable leadership qualities, but also endured many difficult seasons, including divorce and betrayal. She made tough choices but always did her best to care for me.

We can view our past and bloodline through the lens of redemption—God's plan—or through the enemy's attempts at destruction. My mother is an incredible leader with an apostolic anointing to build, teach, and create. The qualities she possesses are a part of my inheritance. They are part of my generational blessings.

After my gold coin dream, God spoke to me about being redemption and destiny-focused. A future focus and "destiny focus" creates momentum and vision, enabling us to step into God's plans. Many people fixate on negative cycles in their family line, but *wherever there is a generational curse, there's an even greater generational blessing.*

I ministered to a woman whose grandfather created the first successful business of its kind. (To protect privacy, I won't name the business.) Her grandfather was a pioneer, but unfortunately, he betrayed many people to achieve his dreams. The woman could view her family story through shame, or she could repent for her grandfather's sins and say, "My grandfather was a pioneer and leader, and God wants to redeem those qualities in me." As we prayed, she recognized that her grandfather's misused gifts were part of her inheritance, even though they were previously used for the enemy's plans instead of God's.

God sent Jesus to redeem and restore what the enemy has stolen—that's the point of Jesus. He redeemed us to God with His blood! We have an inheritance in Jesus, but our view of the past can determine where we can go. Just like me, you can probably see negative qualities in your generational line. I focused on the negative for a long time, but fixating on the devil's destruction shifts our eyes from our destiny. I learned to be destiny and future-focused to step into God's plans. "For I know the plans I have for you," declares the Lord, "plans to prosper you and not to harm you, plans to give you hope and a future" (Jeremiah 29:11).

Rebuilding the Ancient Ruins

Tauren Wells' song "Take It All Back" includes the line, "I'm taking back what the enemy stole." Like me, you can probably see patterns of good and destruction in your generational line and personal life where the enemy has stolen from your destiny. After my gold coin dream, I realized I'd focused on the curses and destruction in my bloodline, but God wanted me to see things from His perspective, which is always: *to restore, redeem, and rebuild the generations.*

God always intends to transform what's broken and hopeless into a testimony of redemption! Isaiah 61:4 says, "They will rebuild the ancient ruins and restore the places long devastated; they will renew the ruined cities that have been devastated for generations." God desires that we rebuild devastated generations. We can reclaim everything the enemy has stolen from our bloodline, including our dreams, and help others do the same.

God's plans are always for good! He is a good Father. The Bible says God is love and sent His Son to die for our sins. Jesus said He came so we could have abundant life, meaning "excessive and overflowing" (John 10:10). God desires His children to live abundantly, not just "survive the workweek." Study the Bible on how God prospers generations, and I believe you'll conclude what I did: *God's plan is always to redeem, restore, and make us new, as if the past never happened.*

God's Plan Is Always Redemption and Restoration

> "For I know the plans I have for you," declares the Lord, "plans to prosper you and not to harm you, plans to give you hope and a future."
> —Jeremiah 29:11

You might wonder how to view your generational line through the lens of redemption. Changing our view of the past changes our future. We can view our past through our own and our family's failures or through God's redemption. *Our family history doesn't define our destiny.*

Paul, formerly Saul, ruthlessly dragged Christians from their homes and had them murdered. Talk about a past that could have defined his future! But God redeemed Saul into Paul, who helped lead the church, walked in the miraculous, and wrote over 60% of the New Testament. Paul's key to breakthrough was staying future-oriented: "Brothers and sisters, I do not regard myself as having taken hold of it yet; but one thing I do: forgetting what lies behind and reaching forward to what lies ahead" (Philippians 3:13). Imagine if Paul let his past define his future.

Another example is the prodigal son. When considering returning home, he said, "I am not worthy," essentially, he believed his future was limited by his past. But when his father received him, he put the best robe, ring, and sandals on him (Luke 15:22). Through this story, God shows that our past doesn't define our future, but we must agree to receive the ring and robe the Father offers. Sometimes, we need to accept this new identity before fully stepping into our destiny. For the prodigal son, putting on the ring and robe meant embracing a redeemed identity.

The story of the prodigal son powerfully depicts the Father redeeming us through Jesus. Jesus paid for every sin—past, present, and future. His blood clears the record of wrongs against us and our family line, making us as white as snow (Isaiah 1:18). We can step into our dreams and live fully alive because of Jesus' precious blood.

Yes, deliverance is sometimes needed when sins lead to demonic habitation. My husband and I were radically delivered years ago, and we often see people set free today. However, our history or need for deliverance doesn't dictate our destiny. Our dreams depend on how we view our past. We must choose to reimagine our past and family history through the lens of redemption, restoration, and inheritance.

The adulterous woman could have let her past define her future. Caught in adultery and brought to Jesus, He told her, "Go and sin no more" (John 8:11). We can view this as a command or as supernatural grace to live a sinless life. When we receive forgiveness for ourselves and extend it to others, we renew our minds through redemption's lens.

If the Apostle Paul had fixated on being a former murderer of Christians and renewed his mind with that identity, he never would have stepped into his destiny. If the prodigal son had dwelled on his past, he wouldn't have accepted the ring and robe. Joseph could have embraced the identity of a betrayed slave, but then he couldn't have become a ruler and second-in-command in Egypt.

Consider other biblical examples. The woman at the well, married five times, became the first evangelist (John 4). Mary Magdalene, once possessed by seven demons, became Jesus' ministry partner and financial supporter (Luke 8:2–3). Peter said to Jesus, "Get away from me, I am a sinful man" (Luke 5:8), yet Jesus chose him to lead His church. Each of these leaders chose to view their past through God's redemption because of Jesus. They let go of their past identities to step into their dreams.

Truly, our past doesn't define our future, nor does our family history define our destiny.

Prophetic Word

You're building a legacy that will bless generations! Your faithfulness today is sowing seeds of God's glory for your family and beyond. He's using you to establish a heritage of faith. Your life reflects His hope, and His plans for you are overflowing (Jeremiah 29:11). You have the faith of Abraham. Like Abraham, you believe God's promises, and your trust is birthing miracles. "He did not waver at the promise of God through unbelief, but was strengthened in faith, giving glory to God." (Romans 4:20)

Truth Declarations

- My family's story is restored, and I walk in the inheritance of God's goodness (Psalm 16:6).
- I speak life over my generations, and my words establish a legacy of hope (Proverbs 18:21).
- God's favor rests on my family, and my children inherit His abundant life (Psalm 112:2).
- My generations are marked by God's faithfulness, and His truth endures through us (Psalm 100:5).
- I release God's healing over my bloodline, and past wounds are transformed into testimonies (Psalm 147:3).

CHAPTER 5

It's Time to Get Going!

"It's not where you start, but whether you start."
—Terri Savelle Foy

I had all the excuses in the world for why I couldn't start doing what God called me to do. I would say things like, *"I don't have enough money or time. I don't know the right people. I don't know how to publish a book. I don't know how to write a book. I don't have enough energy. I'm tired!"*

I've learned that nothing happens when we sit still. For the longest time, I was waiting on God, but God was waiting for me to take steps of faith to move forward. The truth is, we can't wait to feel more anointed, confident, or powerful. If we wait until we "feel ready," we'll never see our dreams come to pass. We have everything we need right now to do what God has called us to do. Throughout this chapter, I'll share five keys to create momentum and move forward so you can take steps toward your dreams.

Key 1 - Quit Making Excuses

The first step for me was to stop making excuses for why I couldn't do what God called me to do. My excuses sounded like this: *"How can I make a podcast when I don't have professional equipment, a microphone, or a studio? How can I write a book when I don't know how? I don't have enough money."* When it came to writing my book, my excuses were, *"I don't have time. I have no formal training. I've never written a book before."* My problem was that I was good at talking myself out of what I was called to do! I had every excuse in the world for why I couldn't take steps forward.

I was busy making excuses and agreeing with reasons why I wouldn't start stepping into my dreams. I had prophetic words about teaching, preaching, leadership, and writing, but I rehearsed the lies that I was unworthy, unqualified, and had nothing significant to say. For most of my life, I believed I could never measure up, so *I reduced my life to the level of my belief system, self-sabotaging my destiny as a result!* I started seeing transformation when I stopped making excuses and intentionally confronted them. This led to taking steps of intentionality, which is my next point.

Key 2 - Intentionality, Action, & Consistency

I've learned that nothing happens unless I do something first. That might seem obvious, but when my dream was to write a book, I had to actually start writing and stop making excuses for why I couldn't write every day. There is power in consistency. I used to wait until I felt like writing to start, but God shows up in the middle of our consistency. I made it a habit to write every day, regardless of how I felt. My consistency brought a major breakthrough in my writing. Instead of waiting for God to show up, I started believing God had anointed me to write the book. He was already with me in the process as I chose to write each day.

Steve Backlund says, "Successful and unsuccessful people both don't feel like doing things, but successful people find a way to do the things they don't feel like doing." Every successful leader knows that what they focus on will grow. There were days when I felt like I was hitting a block, but the illusion of "writer's block" stopped as I renewed my mind with the truth that I had something valuable to say and write, regardless of my feelings. Consistency is a huge key to seeing our dreams fulfilled.

Key 3 – Make Clear Goals

I love the story of Jamie Kern Lima, the creator of *It Cosmetics*. Jamie had a skin condition called rosacea, and she wanted to create a makeup product that worked for women with real skin issues. She wanted to feature "real women" as her models, but beauty industry "experts" told her the idea would never work. One investor even said women would never buy makeup from someone with her body type. Jamie was rejected multiple times, but deep down she knew she'd created something significant with God. Every time she was rejected, she got back up and tried again.

Jamie could have let others' opinions stop her, but she didn't listen to their negativity and kept going. She even said she started viewing rejection differently to stay motivated. Jamie says, "Rejection is God's redirection." Years after launching the company, despite hundreds of rejections, L'Oréal bought It Cosmetics for 1.2 billion dollars. Yes—billions with a "B"! Imagine if she had quit when others called it a bad idea.

I have studied many leaders and what they did to accomplish their goals. They all follow a similar pattern: they have clear goals in mind with deadlines to achieve them. Having clear goals is biblical. Proverbs 29:18 says, "Where there is no prophetic vision, the people perish," and Habakkuk 2:2 says, "Write the vision down." Writing the vision, envisioning what it will look like, and setting clear deadlines helped me reach my goals of writing two books, creating marriage events, and public speaking.

Great questions to ask ourselves are: *What do you want to do, and when do you want it done by?* Clear goals helped me determine what I needed to do each day to reach them. For example, I wanted to write a book but initially had no clear plan. Journaling my goals and target deadlines helped tremendously. I created target dates for my book and when I wanted to hit each milestone. Having clear goals helped me take small steps of faith each day.

Making daily goals also reduced the feeling that the project was overwhelming. Viewing smaller steps eliminated the sense of failure if I didn't write a book in a week. Goals allow us to track progress and celebrate small steps of faith, which brings me to my fourth key: thanksgiving.

Key 4 - Thanksgiving

The enemy always tries to get us to focus on what's not happening. Something that has helped me shift my focus is writing down what I'm thankful for. Part of my daily routine is to write what I'm grateful for each day. I've created a new habit by training myself to start and end my day with gratitude. Something that helps me is what I call "Replace It"—I replace negative thoughts with what I'm grateful for. It's impossible to complain and be grateful at the same time.

What we focus on will grow—if we focus on gratitude, our hearts will be filled with thanksgiving. If we focus on what's seemingly not happening, we'll be filled with doubt, frustration, or fear. It's also important to realize change happens over time, not instantly. As we keep going, regardless of how we feel, we'll see transformation. It's okay when I mess up, and I keep celebrating the steps I've taken to move forward. Gratitude helps us celebrate ourselves as we go through the process.

Key 5 - Surround Yourself with Encouraging People

The enemy will try to intimidate us out of what we're called to do, sometimes using others to discourage and distract us. I mentioned this before, but it's worth repeating. My husband, Pieter, had several well-meaning Christians tell him, "Starting a business from scratch is impossible," but he kept going. Watching Pieter overcome discouragement and others' opinions has been inspirational. Some who told him to quit were medical professionals. Pieter could have easily quit while building our company, Bezalel Innovations. I believe many things in the body of Christ are not built because the enemy causes discouragement.

It's also important to realize that people used by the enemy are not our enemy. Ephesians 6:12 tells us our battle is not with flesh and blood. When well-meaning people tell you to give up on your dreams or quit, it may be because they're justifying why they abandoned their own. Don't hang around discouraging people—they'll drain your energy. They're not bad people, but we must avoid spending time with what I call "bucket takers." Some people fill our buckets with encouragement, love, and wisdom, while others take from our buckets, filling them with discouragement. I want to be a "bucket filler" and a "hope bringer" to others. I believe that's who you are too!

The person who emailed us when we launched our ministry, saying what we were doing was wrong, was not our enemy. I like to say, "If the person is standing in front of you, they are not your enemy." We must remember who our battle is with. The enemy hopes we'll "take the bait" and live offended. Hebrews 12:15 warns that a "root of bitterness" grows when we're offended. I heard John Bevere say the root word for offense is a hunter's trap. Offense literally traps us in the enemy's lies. We can overcome others' negativity by living unoffended, walking in forgiveness, and staying focused on what God has told us to do. What we focus on will grow—we can focus on others' opinions or on what God has called us to do.

I always return to Nehemiah's battle strategy when tempted to quit. Nehemiah received life-threatening letters from government officials when he started rebuilding the walls of Jerusalem. The enemy uses the same strategy today. We received a letter trying to discourage us from starting our ministry and cause us to quit. But I love Nehemiah's response: "Why should I come down to you? I am doing a great work" (Nehemiah 6:3). Nehemiah refused to listen to the enemy or give him a meeting! He kept building and didn't give the enemy the time of day.

The next time you feel discouraged and want to quit, say to the enemy, *"Sorry, I can't come down to you. I'm busy doing a great work for the Lord."*

Prophetic Word

You teach people what it means to live *an abundant life*. God is leading you into a season of abundance and purpose. "The thief does not come except to steal, and to kill, and to destroy. I have come that they may have life, and that they may have it more abundantly." (John 10:10). Your courage inspires others. Your bold steps of faith are a testimony that empowers those around you. "Be strong and of good courage, do not fear nor be afraid of them; for the Lord your God, He is the One who goes with you." (Deuteronomy 31:6)

Truth Declarations

- The Lord is working behind the scenes for my good.
- My prayers move heaven.
- God's promises revive my soul. (Psalm 119:50)
- God's promises never expire.
- Every word God has spoken over my life will come to pass.

CHAPTER 6

Your Work Will Be Rewarded

"But as for you, be strong and do not give up, for your work will be rewarded."

—2 Chronicles 15:7 NIV

David's father, Jesse, sent David on a mission to bring food to his brothers on the battlefield. I believe when David, the future king of Israel, went on this food delivery assignment, he wasn't thinking, "I'm on my way to slay a giant!" He was faithfully stewarding what his father asked him to do. I love that when we're faithful in the little, God promises rewards!

Our "small" tasks today are setting us up for our destiny. David's victories over the lion and bear were his training ground for his prophetic destiny as king of Israel. He privately won many battles before defeating Goliath publicly. "But David said to Saul, 'Your servant has been keeping his father's sheep. When a lion or a bear came and carried off a sheep from the flock, I went after it, struck it, and rescued the sheep from its mouth. When it turned on me, I seized it by its hair, struck it, and killed it. Your servant has killed both the lion and the bear; this uncircumcised Philistine will be like one of them, because he has defied the armies of the living God. The Lord who rescued me from the paw of the lion and the paw of the bear will rescue me from the hand of this Philistine'" (1 Samuel 17:34–37).

You might be in a season where you feel your work isn't significant, but the truth is, your private victories are setting you up for giant breakthroughs. The truth is also that not everyone will see you according to your prophetic destiny. David's father, Jesse, saw him as merely a food delivery service that day. But God sees you and knows you have a significant destiny. The moments of private victory and stewarding the "little" well are leading to public victory. As we faithfully steward our everyday tasks, God sets us up for a huge public victory.

Part of David's strategy in defeating Goliath was declaring the victory before it happened. David believed he could do it, and his declaration backed it up: "This day the Lord will deliver you into my hands, and I'll strike you down and cut off your head." David said to the Philistine, "'You come against me with sword and spear and javelin, but I come against you in the name of the Lord Almighty, the God of the armies of Israel, whom you have defied. This day the Lord will deliver you into my hands, and I'll strike you down and cut off your head. This very day I will give the carcasses of the Philistine army to the birds and the wild animals, and the whole world will know that there is a God in Israel'" (1 Samuel 17:45–46).

Overcoming Perfectionism

I used to think I couldn't be used greatly by God because of my past. I had a subconscious belief that I was limited in what God could do through me. I didn't go to college and had no formal training. I was a stay-at-home mom whose greatest skill was tennis. I thought, "What could God possibly do with my life?" I never imagined I'd be leading a ministry, teaching and preaching at marriage events, or writing a second book! These things seemed impossible.

My view of God was limiting Him. I saw God as a harsh Father. I desperately wanted to please Him, but the perfectionism I thought I needed was causing me to bury my gold coins. Perfectionism stops us from doing anything for God. I didn't believe God loved me regardless of my actions. We bury our talents when we have a faulty view of our heavenly Father. I did this for a long time. My desire to please God was rooted in the lie that I'd be rejected if I failed. Are we viewing our Father as a harsh taskmaster or as someone who loves and is for us?

When we grasp that God, who sent His Son to die for us, loves us completely, we're free to dream, create, and step into our calling. Perfect love casts out all fear (1 John 4:18). To be free from the fear of man, we must renew our minds with the truth that God loves us unconditionally. Children who know they're loved are free to dream, create, and build with God's kingdom. God's love is real, not distant, and it's with us now, regardless of how we feel.

Getting Out of "Survival Mode"

I felt broken when I came to ministry school. As I mentioned before, I was in "survival mode" for most of my life. I had no long-term dreams; I was just trying to survive each day. When I gave my life back to Jesus, it was out of sheer desperation. Unlike my husband's life-shattering salvation encounter, mine was a moment of surrender, like, "I want to do it Your way because my way isn't working." My relationship with God began with just Him and me in my secret place. After my husband left for work, I'd spend hours in God's Word, soaking in the Bible, books, sermons, and teachings.

About three years after my salvation, my husband's affairs came to light one night while we were on vacation in Lake Tahoe. I'd been praying for him, and it felt like nothing was changing. The enemy wants us to feel powerless, like nothing's happening, but it's a lie. I'm sure Abraham had days like that, but God was setting Abraham and Sarah up with perfect timing to birth His promise through Isaac.

"'I will make you a great nation; I will bless you and make your name great; and you shall be a blessing. I will bless those who bless you, and I will curse him who curses you; and in you all the families of the earth shall be blessed'" (Genesis 12:2–3 NKJV).

I now know waiting periods are preparation times to birth God's promises. Waiting seasons aren't punishment; they're divine preparation! This brings me to my next point: you are being divinely set up by God.

You Are Being Set Up

Joseph in Genesis was in prison for 13 years, but at the right time, in the right season, he stood before Pharaoh and became second-in-command of Egypt, just as God promised in his dreams 13 years earlier (Genesis 37:5–9, 41:41–43). God was setting Joseph up for a destiny beyond what he could have asked, thought, or imagined, and that's what God was doing with me—and is doing with you.

God is setting you up for breakthrough, destiny, and fulfilled promises. You might feel abandoned or like you missed it, but God is setting you up! The promises may feel distant, but there are seasons in God, each preparing you for the next. As we take small steps of obedience, we'll see our dreams unfold before our eyes.

Like Joseph, God gave me significant dreams during a season of uncertainty. In one dream, an angel held me as we flew over Israel at night. I saw a city with lights and a crystal-clear river running through it. I'd have impactful dreams, then—nothing would happen. In fact, things seemed to worsen! I felt like Joseph, with prophetic promises but stuck in a pit.

During this waiting season, my dad was diagnosed with cancer, my mom went through a difficult divorce, and my daughter faced a challenging teenage season. My husband was saved, but we were both broken. Every day, the promises felt so far off. I felt like Abraham and Sarah, waiting and wondering if I'd ever birth God's promises.

But God is faithful. During this season, I had a dream where I was at Bethel Church in Redding, California. A beautiful, simple red chair sat at the sanctuary's front. I was naked but not embarrassed, standing by the red chair, and a voice said, "That seat is for you!" I concluded the dream was about attending ministry school in Redding. We sold everything and moved our family there.

After moving to Redding, it seemed nothing was happening. Exhausted and tired, I cried on my carpet out of joy for leaving our old life behind, but we didn't know why we were there. I now know this was a season of preparation and divine setup. The Lord wanted to heal, restore, and make us whole to step into our destiny!

The Lord brought me to Redding to heal from past pain and teach me my identity in Christ. My husband ended up attending ministry school with me for three years. We had no idea God was setting us up to heal our broken hearts so we could walk into His promises! Jesus came to heal the brokenhearted (Luke 4:18). The word "brokenhearted" means a shattered heart. Our hearts were shattered, broken, and wounded. We needed this season to heal. God was setting us up for victory, and even if you can't see the big picture, He's setting you up too.

Dreams Fulfilled

I now work for a pastor at Bethel Church and have been commissioned as a pastor alongside my husband, Pieter. I initially thought my red chair dream was about a seat at ministry school, but I had no idea I'd land my dream job with incredible leaders, Steve and Wendy

Backlund. I never dreamed I'd publish a book, create a course, or build an online school for Steve and Wendy from scratch. I never imagined leading a ministry. But God is the God of divine setup!

God set Esther up in a season of preparation before she was presented to the king. He used this time to prepare her for "such a time as this" (Esther 4:14). Her obedience resulted in the deliverance of the Jewish people from death!

Joseph was prepared for his future during his prison season. When we face difficult seasons, we can let them define us or view them as preparation for what's next. Joseph said, "'You intended to harm me, but God intended it for good to accomplish what is now being done, the saving of many lives'" (Genesis 50:20). His perspective was that the prison season enabled him to rule as second-in-command of Egypt.

God is setting you up to rule and reign too!

Prophetic Word

Your private victories, no matter how small, are preparing you for *giant-slaying* moments! Nothing is holding you back; God's perfect love has set you up for a divine destiny (1 John 4:18). Your work will be rewarded, and He's weaving a story of breakthrough beyond what you can imagine (2 Chronicles 15:7)! God's promises are yes and amen for you. Every word He has spoken over your life will come to pass. "For all the promises of God in Him are Yes, and in Him Amen, to the glory of God through us." (2 Corinthians 1:20)

Truth Declarations

- My faithful work is seen by God, and He rewards my efforts with His abundance (2 Chronicles 15:7).
- I speak life over my tasks, and God's favor transforms my work into blessings (Proverbs 18:21).
- God sees my private victories, and He is setting me up for public reward (Matthew 6:4).
- My efforts are empowered by the Holy Spirit, and God ensures my work prospers (Zechariah 4:6).
- I walk in God's calling, and my faithfulness reaps eternal rewards (1 Corinthians 15:58).

CHAPTER 7

Driven by Destiny

"The devil will give up when he sees you're not going to give in."

—Joyce Meyer

We can be driven by fear, intimidation, and unworthiness, or we can be driven by purpose, vision, and destiny. For most of my life, I was driven by fear instead of by my purpose and vision for my life. Fear is a spirit and a real force against what God has called us to do. I avoided my dreams for a long time because I was fearful of stepping out and felt unworthy. However, the truth is *we won't overcome what we won't confront.*

Kris Vallotton, Senior Pastor and Leader at my home church, Bethel Church, says, "The dogs of doom bark at the door of your destiny." The "dogs," or the enemy, will work overtime to ensure you never believe you have access to dreams, inheritances, blessings, and dreams. I had prophetic words that I would preach, teach, write books, and lead a ministry, but I was allowing the enemy to lie to me and make me feel like I couldn't do it. The enemy was working overtime to intimidate me and steal my confidence. The dogs of doom were barking, saying, "You'll never make it! You're unqualified. You'll never write a book. You're not a good public speaker."

We overcome the enemy by taking steps forward, despite how we feel. As I sat down to write my first book, the enemy would tell me it wouldn't be very good and that no one would read it. There were days when I would give up and stop writing. I was allowing the enemy to send me a message about what I could and could not accomplish with God. The process was frustrating, mostly because I was letting the enemy push me around.

One day, I remember sitting down to write and I would ask God to show me a picture of who needed to read my book and who it would impact. I saw thousands of women reading my books and imagined people being set free from lies as they read them! I envisioned women rising up to do what they're called to do! This prophetic picture gave me a clear vision to keep going and step into my dreams.

As I mentioned in an earlier chapter, a clear vision is key to resisting the enemy. Without a clear vision of the "why" and the "who" our dreams will impact, we'll want to quit and give in to the enemy's lies. Others are waiting for us to do that thing God has called us to do. I'm using my book as an example, but your dream could be to start a business, pursue a degree, or launch a ministry. Whatever it is, keeping a picture of who needs you to step into your dreams will keep you motivated. Intimidation might be knocking at your door, but the Bible says we resist the devil, and he will flee from us (James

4:7). We resist by keeping the vision and God's promises in front of us as we take courageous steps of faith forward.

Spiritual Bootcamp

During the season when I was overcoming intimidation and fear, I had a dream one night. In the dream, I was alone and trying to enter a 40-day bootcamp in the mountains and I had to report to a woman holding a clipboard. The woman would frown and scowl at me saying "You aren't strong enough for this bootcamp." She looked at her clipboard and back at me and had me lift my arms to show my muscles (or rather, my lack of muscles) and said, "You'll never make it." Something rose up inside me, and I shouted back, "I am strong enough! I am doing this bootcamp!" Then, the woman allowed me to enter the bootcamp, and I woke up.

Bootcamps push you to your maximum capacity. They're where weak people enter but come out stronger on the other side. God was showing me that it wouldn't always be easy, but I was strong enough to do what He was calling me to do. The truth was, I had started shrinking back from my calling because I was partnering with intimidation, and I was burying my talents as a result. The bootcamp dream was a wakeup call!

Each of us has a unique assignment and anointing to do what God has called us to do. The anointing is the presence and person of the Holy Spirit upon our lives to accomplish God's calling. My problem wasn't a lack of resources, time, money, or anointing; my problem was my lack of "yes." We say yes first, and then God brings what we need—not the other way around. I had to face the fact that I was allowing the enemy to speak to me about my calling. I was listening to his lies: "You're not smart enough, brave enough, anointed enough, strong enough..." I had to face the fact that God wanted to strengthen me, but I had to say yes first.

Spirits of Intimidation

There are literal spirits of fear and intimidation that will try to get us to quit and give up on our dreams. Lisa Bevere recently shared a story online about the first time she preached in a church. When the congregation realized a woman was going to preach, about 150 of the 200 attendees stood up and left. After they left, with just 50 people in the audience, Lisa still stepped out and preached the message. Her husband, John, was out of town, and that night, while Lisa was home, one of the church attendees came banging on her door to tell her she shouldn't preach. It was so intense that Lisa had to call the police to get the person to leave!

Lisa said she knew she was up against a spirit of intimidation trying to get her to quit and back down from her future as a preacher. She admitted she wanted to quit after the incident. Lisa says, "Intimidation will shut down the gift of God on your life faster than anything else." Intimidation will try to make you shrink back from your calling and give up. 2 Timothy 1:7 says, "God has not given us a spirit of fear, but of power and of love and of a sound mind." Look at what Matthew 10:26-27 says in The Message translation: "Don't be intimidated. Eventually everything is going to be out in the open, and everyone will know how things really are. So don't hesitate to go public now."

Intimidation is the voice of the enemy, trying to get us to give up and cower in fear.

Overcoming Fear and Intimidation

I had my own battle against intimidation when I started preaching for the first time. It's important to realize the enemy will use people to intimidate us and get us to quit. One time, right before I was about to preach at our first in-person marriage event, a man approached me to complain about a deliverance session his wife had with me and another minister. I was literally walking up to take the stage when he confronted me. He had been at the event for two days, yet he chose that moment to speak to me. Not only did he confront me, but he pointed a finger in my face!

I interrupted him and told him I could not talk now. I got up on stage and tried to shake off the accusations. The man's wife had never reached out to me personally to discuss her concerns, so I was shocked by his words, especially since I had never heard concerns directly from his wife. The Lord spoke to me clearly as I walked onto the stage: "Melinda, this is a spirit of intimidation trying to intimidate you right before you preach." The enemy will use anything and anyone to try to stop us from stepping into what we're called to do.

Let's look at the strategy of intimidation sent against Elijah. Elijah was threatened by the enemy and bullied by the enemy, and as a result he became afraid and ran for his life. "Now Ahab told Jezebel everything Elijah had done and how he had killed all the prophets with the sword. So Jezebel sent a messenger to Elijah to say, 'May the gods deal with me, be it ever so severely, if by this time tomorrow I do not make your life like that of one of them.' When he came to Beersheba in Judah, he left his servant there, while he himself went on a day's journey into the wilderness. He came to a broom bush, sat down under it and prayed that he might die. 'I have had enough, Lord,' he said. 'Take my life; I am no better than my ancestors.' Then he lay down under the bush and fell asleep" (1 Kings 19:1–5).

Jezebel intimidated Elijah right out of his destiny! Jezebel has many functions, but she is primarily a spirit of intimidation. Her demonic influence was strong enough to get a prophet of God to hide in a cave after he had defeated the prophets of Baal. Jezebel is still active today, and while I don't like to focus on the enemy, we need to be aware that this spirit will try to stop us and use others to make us want to quit. We must recognize when the enemy sends assignments of intimidation against us.

Most people would have had no idea I was battling so much fear of man and intimidation during my early speaking sessions. I would preach and teach, then immediately feel like it wasn't good enough. Preaching this way was exhausting! Instead of celebrating that I had stepped out, I was condemning myself for not measuring up. I felt so tired during this season, and there were days I just wanted to quit! I had no idea that what I was really up against was a spirit of intimidation.

I overcame my battle with fear and intimidation by taking steps forward each day, regardless of how I felt. Remember my bootcamp dream? God was training me to be strong and reliant on His anointing upon my life. *Muscles grow by pushing against resistance.* God was teaching me how to resist the devil and step into what He called me to do. I had to press against resistance and build "spiritual muscles." Practically this meant I had to refuse to hide out in a cave like Elijah, and take steps forward each day. You don't get strong by working out just once. God was teaching me the power of consistency. I had to wake up and make a decision to do what He called me to do every day. Since releasing our marriage restoration testimony publicly at marriage events and conferences, we've had many couples and individuals reach out for help and many marriages have been restored!

When the Enemy Taunts You

We overcome the lies of the enemy, not just by starting, but by completing what God has called us to do. I receive messages all the time about how my book has impacted people. I always think to myself, *What if I had quit and given in to the enemy's lies?*

The enemy is a bully, and he wants us to quit. One of my favorite lines in the Bible is in the book of Nehemiah. I love how Nehemiah responded to the threats of the enemy. Nehemiah was being bullied, and he even received death threats as he was doing what he was called to do—rebuild the walls of Jerusalem. Nehemiah said to his enemies, "I am carrying on a great project and cannot go down. Why should the work stop while I leave it and go down to you?" (Nehemiah 6:3, author paraphrase). Nehemiah responded the way we all need to when the enemy comes whispering, "Your idea will never work"

- "Sorry, why should I come down to you? I'm busy doing a great work for the Lord."

I want to share three keys that have helped me overcome the spirit of intimidation. The first step is to do it afraid. We can't wait for our feelings to be right before we step out and do something. I had to preach even though I was afraid. We gain momentum in the spiritual realm by moving forward. Whenever I feel like quitting, I go back to my prophetic word: "Melinda, if you don't quit, you win." Now say the same thing over yourself, adding your name: "[Your name], if you don't quit, you win!"

Galatians 6:9 says, "Let us not become weary in doing good, for at the proper time we will reap a harvest if we do not give up." God promises we'll reap a harvest if we don't give up. My bootcamp dream and gold coin dream revealed the reality of what was happening to me. The dogs of doom were barking at the doors of my destiny, but I knew would be victorious if I didn't give up.

The second step to overcoming fear and intimidation is to realize that our feelings are not the truth. You might feel intimidated, but James 4:7 says we can resist the devil, and he will flee from us. Moving forward, despite how we feel, is the key to breakthrough. Jesus said, "My yoke is easy and my burden is light" (Matthew 11:30), so as we rely on Jesus to do what God has called us to do, it takes the pressure off. Our feelings will change as we rely on Jesus and His anointing on our lives and as we move forward despite how we feel.

The final step is to stay thankful. Thanksgiving is a huge key to overcoming intimidation and fear. It's difficult to focus on fear while staying in a posture of gratitude. Psalm 8:2 says that our praises silence the enemy. Praise is one of our biggest weapons as we move forward to step into our dreams. Your intentional praise will silence the enemy. Watch the enemy flee as you praise God and step boldly into your dreams!

Lastly, I want to repeat what I said before: You have a calling, an assignment, and a significant destiny. The question to ask yourself is the same one I had to ask myself: Will I cower in fear, or will I say to the enemy when he taunts me, "Sorry, I cannot come down to you; I'm busy doing a great work for the Lord"?

Prophetic Word

You have stepped into a new season of boldness, clarity, courage and confidence. You are an overcomer who is making a significant impact in the world. God has not given you a spirit of fear (timidity), He has given you *His Spirit* full of power, love and a sound mind. The testimony of what you have overcome is going to significantly impact the generations. You were born for such a time as this (Esther 4:14)!

Truth Declarations

- I am chosen, called, and appointed. (John 15:16)
- God will bring it to pass. (Psalm 37:5)
- I am filled with God's perfect love, and it casts out all fear in my heart (1 John 4:18).

- I walk in boldness because the Holy Spirit empowers me to do all God has called me to (2 Timothy 1:7).
- Fear has no hold on me, for I am free in Christ's truth (John 8:32).

CHAPTER 8

The Power of Forgiveness to Step Into Your Dreams

> "Forgiveness positions us to step into the palace to rule and reign."
>
> —Melinda Lagaay

Nothing will prevent us from stepping into our dreams like unforgiveness and bitterness. I know this personally because I was betrayed by my husband when his affairs came out years ago. I've experienced some of the most heartbreaking pain, and if you're reading this, I know you probably have been betrayed before too. Your story might be different from mine, but most of us can say we have been betrayed or hurt by someone close to us. The problem is, unforgiveness keeps us in a mental prison that prevents us from stepping into our dreams. We might be physically free, but we can still be trapped in unresolved pain and unforgiveness. Maybe you feel like I did when my husband's affairs came out, or perhaps you can relate to Joseph in the book of Genesis, who found himself in prison after being betrayed by his own brothers.

I love the story of Joseph because it demonstrates what God can do through someone who is willing to forgive. Joseph could have lost hope while he was in a prison. The Bible says he was "bound in fetters and chains," but despite his horrible circumstances, God still planned for Joseph to become a significant ruler in Egypt. God intended to elevate and promote Joseph right in front of those who betrayed him, but it was Joseph's forgiveness and his *perspective* about the betrayal he experienced that would ultimately determine if he was ready to rule and reign.

Let's continue looking at the story of Joseph and pick up when Joseph was reunited with his brothers thirteen years later after they had sold him into slavery. There was a severe famine in the land and Joseph's brothers came to Egypt looking for food. By that time, Joseph had been moved to the palace as second in command of all of Egypt. Joseph's brothers came to the palace looking to buy food, but they had no idea that their little brother was now in charge of running the palace. Joseph chose to hide his identity, but after sending his brothers back and forth, Joseph finally chose to reveal his identity to his brothers.

This is what Joseph said to his brothers the moment his identity was revealed. "I am Joseph!' ... whom you sold into slavery in Egypt. But don't be upset, and don't be angry with yourselves for selling me to this place. *It was God who sent me here ahead of you to preserve your lives... God has sent me ahead of you to keep you and your families alive and to preserve many survivors.* So it was God who sent me here, not you! And He is the one who made me an adviser to Pharaoh—the manager of his entire palace and the governor of all Egypt" (author's emphasis Genesis 45:4–8).

The key to Joseph's breakthrough was viewing his brothers' betrayal as a divine setup. I believe Joseph understood the impact his intentional forgiveness would have on his destiny when he chose to forgive his brothers. *Joseph's conclusion about his past, present, and future was that it was all orchestrated by God to prosper him and future generations.*

Jesus said we are to bless those who curse us and pray for those who spitefully use us. Joseph's response to forgiving his brothers demonstrated that he could be trusted by God to step into his dream to rule and reign. Not only did Joseph choose not to retaliate against his brothers, but he took care of them and their children. Years later, when Joseph's father passed away, Joseph had another opportunity to retaliate, but he extended mercy to his brothers when justice was due. Here is Joseph's incredible response to his brothers who were worried Joseph was going to have repaid for what they did after their father died:

"'Don't be afraid of me. Am I God, that I can punish you? You intended to harm me, but *God intended it all for good.* He brought me to this position so I could save the lives of many people. No, don't be afraid. I will continue to take care of you and your children.' So he reassured them by speaking kindly to them" (Genesis 50:19–21).

We can't rule in the palace with a prisoner's mindset.

Joseph had the heart and mindset of someone God could trust to lead. *We can't rule in the palace with a prisoner's mindset.* Bitterness keeps us in a mental prison. I love that Joseph refused to let his past circumstances define his prophetic destiny. I believe he knew bitterness would hold him back from his calling. God had big plans for Joseph, and he couldn't let bitterness obstruct what God planned to do through his life.

Joseph chose to release his brothers from all responsibility for their actions, instead of retaliating for his pain. The result was God promoting Joseph to a palace. Joseph was *destiny-oriented, not past-oriented.* Jesus illustrates unforgiveness in the parable of the unforgiving servant, saying we'd be "delivered to the torturers" if we refuse to forgive (Matthew 18:34–35). Torturers are demonic spirits—unforgiveness invites torment into our hearts and minds! Bitterness is the manifestation of prolonged, untreated unforgiveness (Hebrews 12:15).

The devil wants to destroy our destiny, marriages, ministries, churches, children, families, and relationships through bitterness and unforgiveness, but Joseph understood that forgiveness wasn't just for him—it was for the generations!

Forgiving for Infidelity

Forgiving Pieter was the hardest thing I've ever done, but forgiveness set me free from mental torment. It allowed me to experience authentic peace, happiness, and joy. Forgiveness also allowed me to step into my destiny to help others forgive for really difficult things. Imagine if I'd stayed bitter toward Pieter—unforgiveness would have robbed me of my destiny. The beautiful part of my story is that God removed the pain from my past once I gave it to Jesus. We weren't meant to live with unresolved pain. Though it was hard, I knew allowing Pieter's affairs to linger in my heart would invite demonic torment. Forgiveness isn't an obligation; it's freedom for our hearts and minds and extends supernatural grace to the offender to be set free.

I not only forgave Pieter, but also the women he had affairs with and I blessed them too. Anyone who has affairs desperately needs Jesus' mercy and grace. Forgiving infidelity may seem offensive until we realize we were all sinners before Jesus. We all need God's mercy, love, and grace. Our Father sent Jesus to die to extend grace to the worst sinners. Pieter and I were the worst sinners, yet our merciful King saw a broken couple needing His grace, love, and mercy. That's what grace is—mercy when we don't deserve it.

I'm not saying we shouldn't establish boundaries or allow repeated harm. Sometimes, tough decisions are needed when people continually hurt us. Extending mercy must be received, and the fruit of receiving it is not repeatedly hurting the person who extended it. When mercy isn't received, healthy boundaries are necessary.

The Pardon of Forgiveness

Forgiveness, as defined in Strong's Concordance, is "a dismissal, release, pardon; releasing someone from an obligation and a debt. The excusing of an offense without exacting a penalty, a release from the legal penalties of an offense, an official warrant of remission of penalty, a royal pardon... excuse or forgiveness for a fault or offense." Forgiveness is issuing a pardon in the spirit realm by declaring, "I no longer hold you responsible for what you did to me."

Bitterness literally prevents us from stepping into our destiny. I call it a "destiny destroyer." *We can't take the past into our destiny!* The Bible says the word of the Lord tested Joseph's character (Psalm 105:19), and he passed the test! His intentional forgiveness of betrayal created a massive breakthrough for him and his entire generational bloodline. Like Jesus with the adulterous woman, Joseph refused to throw stones at his brothers, extending mercy instead of judgment.

I was deeply betrayed when Pieter's infidelity and pornography addiction surfaced. I discovered his affairs through a text on Pieter's phone. I was shocked and devastated, unaware he was unfaithful. You might recall a similar moment in your life. Yes, I was victimized, but I had to refuse to live like a victim. A victim mentality allows the enemy to rob us of our destiny. The gold coins from my dream from Chapter 1, represented what the Father planned to do through my life—the coins represented my generational inheritance, my dreams, and my prophetic destiny.

During the weeks after the affairs surfaced, the Lord spoke to me about the generational impact of bitterness and unforgiveness. He said to my heart, "Melinda, bitterness is bondage, but forgiveness is freedom!" Hebrews 12:15 tells us that a root of bitterness defiles us. Bitterness is poison to our souls. The Lord said, "Melinda, forgiveness has the power to set an entire generation free."

The question is this: *Will we forgive so an entire generation can benefit, or will we hold bitterness toward those who have hurt us?* Your intentional forgiveness is setting you up to step into your destiny and will set an entire generation free!

Our Enemy Is Not Flesh and Blood

Our enemy is not flesh and blood—our enemy is the devil, not people. The enemy uses people to hurt us, but like Joseph, we must realize they're being used by the devil. Why does the enemy try so hard to enter a body? Because, *his only power is in human agreement.* We can reclaim our power and authority through intentional forgiveness. *Forgiveness literally destroys the devil's plans!* Forgiveness is one of the most powerful weapons available to believers in God's kingdom, and the devil knows it. He hopes we won't wield it. Forgiveness isn't just saying, "I forgive you," or a feeling we stir up. It's a pardon, dismissal, and release in the spirit realm. Forgiveness destroys the enemy's works and removes his legal right to harass us.

Forgiveness is more than releasing the person to Jesus—it's dismantling the lies the enemy caused us to believe due to past events. When my husband's affairs surfaced, I forgave him, but I didn't realize I still believed lies about those events. The lies and vows (inner agreements) in my heart held me back from God's fullness for me.

The lies I faced included: "You deserved what happened because of your past sins. God is withholding from you because of what you did. You must care for everyone else. You're not a good Christian. You're not a good wife." Vows are tied to lies with a "therefore" attached, like, "I'm not a good Christian, therefore, God is mad at me and holding out on me."

Lies and vows sound absurd when spoken aloud, but they often reside in our subconscious. They're subtle, but the enemy wants us to feed on them because he knows the truth sets us free. Living under lies and vows limited what God could do in my life. The Lord said to my heart, "We can only have breakthrough at the level of our belief systems." "As a man thinks in his heart, so is he" (Proverbs 23:7).

Maybe, like me, you've been deeply betrayed or hurt. Perhaps that person can't remain in your life because they're dangerous. I've ministered to hundreds of people, and some cannot maintain contact with those who brutally abused them. I understand, but we can offer a pardon. The pardon of forgiveness releases the offender and us. Freedom and peace come when we pardon those who hurt us most.

Prophetic Word

Your intentional forgiveness of others and yourself is setting you up for a generational breakthrough. Your life will be marked with favor, blessings, and inheritance. Your forgiveness will create breakthroughs for you and your entire generational line. You are a radical forgiver! You are a kingdom leader who will significantly impact generations. I see family restoration and wounds healing as you release others to Jesus. Your intentional forgiveness is opening a door to step into your God-sized dreams!

Truth Declarations

- I choose forgiveness, and God's love heals every wound in my heart (Psalm 147:3).
- My forgiveness reflects God's heart, and it opens doors to His restoration (Matthew 6:14–15).
- I am fully forgiven by God's grace, and my past is washed clean by Jesus' blood (Ephesians 1:7).
- I forgive others and myself easily.
- My intentional forgiveness creates well-being for me and others.

Section two of this book contains the forgiveness prayer.

CHAPTER 9

The Time is Now

> "For if you remain silent at this time, relief and deliverance for the Jews will arise from another place, but you and your father's family will perish. And who knows but that you have come to your royal position for such a time as this?"
>
> —Esther 4:14

I had a dream where I heard the unimaginable sounds of hell. It began with me standing in a small hardware store alongside a prayer team. Tools hung on the walls. I knelt as the team prayed, ministering to a young man lying facedown on the floor. He was dragging himself away from the group with his arms, but I pulled him back by his legs, shouting, "Jesus loves you! Jesus loves you! Jesus loves you!" Finally, he stopped fighting, and without words, I knew he had surrendered his life to Jesus.

After this, I stood and walked around the corner to another room in the shop. I found myself alone before a doorway with no door, only blackness beyond. I knew it was a portal. Suddenly, horrific sounds came from the black portal, and I instantly recognized them: "I am hearing the sounds of hell." The sounds were the most demonic, evil noises I'd ever heard—inhuman. Then I woke up.

I awoke knowing the young man had been pulled out of hell. As children of God, we are created to carry God's love, power, and heart to a broken world. We're called to pull others from a future in hell. For too long, I let fear, intimidation, and timidity hold me back from helping others. I knew God was calling me to write this book, but for a season, I allowed the enemy's lies to stop me.

The dream of hell showed me it was about more than just me—the next generation was counting on me! I had a calling to pull others from hell into Jesus' love, and so do you! The tools in the dream symbolized that I had all the "tools" needed to fulfill my dreams. You, too, are fully equipped to do what God has called you to do. You are equipped to step into your dreams! The anointing on your life is the Holy Spirit, empowering you to do what only you can, in a way only you can. I want to finish by sharing three truths that have helped me step into my dreams, and I know they will be a blessing to you too.

Key 1 - You are Strong and Courageous

Stepping into Your God-Sized Dreams requires courage, but *courage is not a feeling*. Courage is a decision to take steps forward every day. Any dream worth pursuing with the Lord is going to require choosing courage over fear. Joshua's calling was a God-sized dream. God promised Joshua he was going to lead the people into the promised land, yet God told him to have courage because there was going to be a battle to take possession of the land.

The battle was primarily for Joshua's *perspective*. There was an inheritance on the other side of the Jordan river, but Joshua had to take steps forward to possess his dreams. Would he continue to trust God and believe he had given him possession of the land, or would he cower in fear?

I love Joshua 21:45 which says, not a single thing the Lord promised to the children of Israel failed. God kept *all* of his promises! Joshua's dreams fulfilled not only brought him into the promised land, but Joshua brought an entire generation with him. You too, are strong and courageous. You are taking territory for the Lord that is going to benefit *the generations.*

Key 2 - You Have Authority

> "And having disarmed the powers and authorities, he made a public spectacle of them, triumphing over them by the cross."
>
> —Colossians 2:15 NIV

I have led many deliverances with my husband, and my favorite part is listening to people describe what they are seeing during the deliverance session. People will often see a "big powerful" demon at the beginning of the deliverance. However, by the end of the deliverance, they will describe the demon again, and will say the appearance of the demon has changed to reflect a small "mouse-sized" demon. The interesting part is the demon was never very powerful, but God showed the person a new perspective about their own authority..

When the person has the revelation that the demonic spirit is really powerless over them, they get free! I have seen this happen time and time again in the deliverance ministry. People have the revelation, they are not victims to the devil. *The devil is a victim to them!*

The triumphant procession is the reality of what happened to the enemy when Jesus defeated him on the cross. God literally made a public spectacle of the enemy through Jesus! The enemy was defeated through the power of the blood of Jesus, and the resurrection! Not only did Jesus lead the enemy into a triumphant procession, but he gave children of God power over all the works of the enemy! "Behold! I have given you authority and power to trample upon serpents and scorpions, and [physical and mental strength and ability] over all the power that the enemy [possesses]; and nothing shall in any way harm you." Luke 10:19 AMPC.

It is important to remember that *the enemy cannot stop you from doing what God has said you can do.* I recently watched an interview with a former satanist who was saved through a radical encounter with Jesus. The former satanist described how the devil comes after believers, and he said one of the first things they do is to try to get Christians to doubt their *authority*.

We have authority, but we can give it up if we believe somehow the enemy can stop us from stepping into the dreams God has given to us. Spiritual warfare is primarily a battle for *perspective.* As we step out into our dreams and take territory for the Lord, we can be assured that we are fighting *from victory and for victory!*

Key 3 - You are Heaven's Answer!

Steve Backlund says, "God's answer to problems is always a leader." *You are that leader!* You have an assignment from heaven! Every person has a unique and significant calling. The question is: Will we arise in this hour and step into our dreams? As leaders for the kingdom of God, if we don't rise up and step out, *who will?*

You are called, anointed, and chosen. Like Esther, you were born for such a time as this. You are heaven's answer and God is excited to partner with you in fulfilling the God-Dreams of your life! Are you ready? This is your time!

Prophetic Word

As I wrote this book, I heard this phrase repeatedly in my spirit: **It's GO Time! It's GO Time! It's GO Time!** It's time to step into what you were called to do, and embrace the dreams God has placed in your heart so the next generation can reap the benefits. You were designed to make an impact and created for greatness. You are surrounded with favor. God's favor is opening doors no one can shut for your destiny. "For You, O Lord, will bless the righteous; with favor You will surround him as with a shield." (Psalm 5:12). God's favor is surrounding you! God is with you, mighty warrior!

Ready, set, GO!

Truth Declarations

- I am born for this moment, and God's purpose flows through me now (Esther 4:14).
- I carry God's anointing, uniquely positioned to shine His light today (Matthew 5:16).
- My life aligns with God's perfect timing, and I walk in His divine plan (Ecclesiastes 3:1).
- I am chosen for this season, and my gifts impact the world for Christ (1 Peter 2:9).
- God's Spirit empowers me to fulfill my calling in this hour (Philippians 4:13).
- I was created to make an impact.
- With God, all things are possible!

The next section of the book contains activations to step into your dreams.

Ready, Set, GO!

PART 2

The Dare to Dream Again Activations: *Practical steps to create momentum, take action, and step into your God-Sized Dreams.*

The 6-Step Dare to Dream Again Process

Step 1: Dare to Dream Again
Step 2: Get a Vision for Your Dream
Step 3: See Who Your Dream Will Impact
Step 4: Forgive, Release, and Bless
Step 5: Plan, Action, and Movement
Step 6: Completion of the Dream

Step 1: Dare to Dream Again

Let's take time right now to start to *Dream Again* with God. What dreams are on your heart to accomplish with God? Ask God for a picture and write down what you see. If you feel stuck, ask God to show you a picture of your dreams. Write down the first thing you see.

Ask yourself this question: If there were absolutely no limits to what I could do, what would I want to accomplish with God? Write down your dreams as if you knew they were *limitless*.

Ask yourself these questions: Who do I have compassion for? Who do I feel called to help? What have I overcome personally that I can help others overcome?

What are some of the gifts and talents in yourself? What are the talents in your generational family line that have been passed down to you?

Step 2: Get a Vision for Your Dream

Write down *at least 10 dreams* you want to accomplish over the next five years.

After you listed the 10 dreams above, what dream will you start today? Of all the dreams you wrote down, what is the dream that gets you the most excited? What dream could be accomplished within one year?

_____
_____
_____
_____
_____
_____
_____

What is one dream you have chosen to focus on and cast a vision for?

_____
_____
_____
_____
_____
_____
_____
_____

Imagine you have already accomplished your dream above. What does it look like to see the dream or hold it in your hands? What does it feel like? What does it look like? How are others being impacted by your dream? Imagine you are living in the dream. Write down what you see.

Step 3: See Who Your Dream Will Impact

Now that you have your one dream you are going to focus on, we are going to ask ourselves some key questions. Let's imagine you are standing in your dream. Who has been impacted by your dream? Who's life has been transformed because you said yes to your dream?

Ask yourself this question: What problem will my dream help others solve? Write down what you see.

Step 4: Forgive, Release, and Bless

Sit with the Holy Spirit and list those you need to forgive—perhaps yourself or others. Go through the forgiveness prayer below and list "truths" the Lord speaks to you. Write down what you see, hear, sense, know, or feel.

Where can you see patterns of generational unforgiveness and bitterness in your family? What was the effect of the prolonged unforgiveness?

_____
_____
_____
_____
_____
_____
_____
_____
_____

Who is God putting on your heart to forgive (if anyone)?

_____
_____
_____
_____
_____
_____
_____
_____
_____

Forgiveness Steps

1. Release and let go
2. Identify the lies
3. Identify the vows
4. Discover the truth
5. Renounce the lie and vow
6. Declare the truth
7. Turn the truth into a declaration!

Forgiveness Prayer

1. Release and let go: Jesus, I choose to forgive _____ for what they did to me. I release them to you.

2. Identify the Lies: Jesus, what lies was I caused to believe about myself (identity/purpose/ability statements) from this circumstance? You might see a picture or hear a word or sense something.

3. Identify the Vows: Jesus, what were the vows I agreed to because of these lies? (Vows are inner agreements). Example: I am never enough (lie), therefore I will stop trying (vow).

4. Discover the Truth through an Encounter: "Jesus, I don't want to believe these lies anymore. Your word is the truth and sanctifies me. Jesus, What is the truth that you would speak into my heart over this situation?"

5. Renounce Lie and Vow: Jesus, in your name and by your blood, I renounce the enemy's accusations and lies I believed when I said in my heart _____(state all the lies and vows).

6. Declare the Truth: I now choose to believe the truth of what you spoke when you said _____ (state all the truths – try to get several!).

7. Turn the truth into several powerful declarations! Here are a few examples: The Father loves me! I am powerful! I am anointed! I carry the love and power of God! I am in God's perfect timing! My body is thriving! My mind is powerful and sound! I have the Holy Spirit living inside of me! I am worthy of love!

The most important part of forgiveness is the truth revealed! The past does not define your destiny. What is the truth you will believe and declare as you move forward?

Write your new Truth Declarations here and say them out loud daily:

_____

_____

_____

_____

_____

_____

Now it's time to bless the person who caused you pain. Say the person's name out loud and bless them. (Even if you cannot have a relationship with the person who hurt you, we can still bless them).

_____
_____
_____
_____
_____
_____
_____
_____
_____

What is the impact of your intentional forgiveness on the other person? What is the impact forgiveness will have on your destiny? Write down what you see.

_____
_____
_____
_____
_____
_____
_____

Step 5: Plan, Action, and Movement

What are some excuses you have made that are preventing you from stepping into your dream? (Example: I don't have time, money, resources, etc.) What is one thing you can start doing today to step into your dream? (Share your dream with a trusted friend, start doing research, start writing, etc).

___

What are the small tasks you are doing today that are leading to a big reward? What are you stewarding today, so that you can step into your dream? (Maybe it's your current job, a business, a ministry, raising your children, etc.)

___

What are practical steps you can take each day to move forward into your dream? (Write for 20 minutes each day, record one podcast per week, etc.)

___

What clear goals do you need to have each day, week, and month, in order to accomplish your dream? (Example: I wanted to write a book in 6 months, so I had to write 1 chapter per week in order to have my book edited, published, and available for readers to buy within 6 months). Get specific and write down exactly when you will need to take each step.

___

Get more specific: What do you need to do *every single day* to accomplish your dream? (Example: I need to write 2 pages or 250 words per day to have a book published in 6 months).

How can you practically add the above step into your daily schedule? (Example: I am going to get up 20 minutes early or go to bed and write instead of scrolling on my phone). How will you track your progress? (Daily journal, etc.)

Gratitude is a key to stepping into our dreams. What are you thankful for right now? What dream can you be thankful for before it happens? What are some ways you can incorporate thanksgiving into your daily routine?

_____
_____
_____
_____
_____
_____
_____
_____

Who has God put in your life that will encourage and inspire you? What kind of people would you like to be around?

_____
_____
_____
_____
_____
_____
_____
_____

Step 6: Completion of the Dream

What will it look like to hold your *completed dream?* If your dream is something you can't physically hold, what will it look like to hold a representation of the dream? (Example: If your dream is to buy and remodel a house for your family, what would it feel like to hold the key? What would it feel like to hold the book in your hands that you wrote?)

_____
_____
_____
_____
_____

Let's review: Who will be impacted because you said yes to your dream?

_____
_____
_____
_____
_____
_____

How would you feel after accomplishing your dream? How do you feel after completing your dream?

_____

_____

_____

_____

_____

_____

_____

Dream Declarations

I am God's masterpiece. "I am God's handiwork, created in Christ Jesus to do good works" (Ephesians 2:10, NIV).

I embrace my God-sized dreams, trusting nothing is impossible with God. "With God all things are possible" (Matthew 19:26, NIV).

I am anointed and gifted to impact others through my dreams. "I have been anointed by the Holy One and know the truth" (1 John 2:20, NIV).

I refuse to let my past define my future, stepping boldly into my calling. "I am a new creation; the old has gone, the new has come!" (2 Corinthians 5:17, NIV).

I dream big because God has big plans for me. "I know the plans God has for me, plans to prosper me and give me a future" (Jeremiah 29:11, NIV).

I step boldly into my dreams, knowing I'm equipped by the Holy Spirit.

"I am filled with the Spirit of God, with wisdom and understanding" (Ephesians 5:18, NIV).

It's GO Time! I arise to impact the next generation with my dreams. "I am born for such a time as this, to do God's work" (Esther 4:14, NIV).

I pass my baton to others, empowering them through my dreams. "I am called to be a blessing to all the families of the earth" (Genesis 12:3, NKJV).

I take risks for my dreams, trusting God's abundant life for me. "I have come that they may have life, and have it to the full" (John 10:10, NIV).

I surround myself with encouragers who see my prophetic potential. "I walk with the wise and become wise" (Proverbs 13:20, NIV).

I say "yes" to God's call – I am ready! "I am ready, for the Lord equips those He calls" (Hebrews 13:21, NIV).

I boldly pursue the dreams God has ignited in me.

"I trust in the Lord, and He directs my paths" (Proverbs 3:5–6, NIV).

My future is greater than my past, and I'm moving forward now.

"I am transformed, for old things have passed away" (2 Corinthians 5:17, NKJV).

I record my vision clearly and run toward it with faith.

"I write the vision; I engrave it plainly to run with it" (Habakkuk 2:2, NASB).

I declare the dreams God has put in my heart with bold confidence.

"I speak, and my words establish God's purpose" (Job 22:28, ESV).

I am crafted uniquely to fulfill God's assignment for me.

"I am God's masterpiece, created for His purpose" (Ephesians 2:10, NLT).

I take daily steps toward my dreams, trusting God's plan.

"I delight in the Lord, and He establishes my steps" (Psalm 37:23, NIV).

I connect with faith-filled people who champion my vision.

"I choose friends who build my faith" (Hebrews 10:24–25, NIV).

I reject all fear of the future and embrace my God-given destiny.

"I am bold, for God has given me a spirit of power" (2 Timothy 1:7, NIV).

I see my dreams thriving in my mind before they unfold.

"I hold fast to God's vision, for it brings life" (Proverbs 29:18, ESV).

I am destined for greatness, walking in God's call.

"I am chosen to bear fruit that lasts" (John 15:16, NIV).

I walk confidently in the purpose God has for me.

"I am guided by the Lord, who goes before me" (Deuteronomy 31:8, NIV).

My faith in God opens doors no one can shut.

"I believe, and all things are possible with God" (Mark 9:23, NIV).

I rely on God to complete His work in my life.

"I am confident God will fulfill His purpose for me" (Psalm 138:8, NIV).

I am equipped by God's grace, not limited by my past.

"I am called and anointed by God" (1 John 2:27, NIV).

I speak words of faith that align with God's truth.

"I choose words that bring life and blessing" (Proverbs 18:21, ESV).

I expect God's blessings to overflow in my life.

"I trust God is doing a new thing in me" (Isaiah 43:19, NIV).

I am fearless, stepping into my calling with God's power.

"I am like a lion, bold in the Lord's strength" (Proverbs 28:1, NIV).

I trust God's might to conquer every challenge I face.

"The Lord is my rock and my deliverer" (Psalm 18:2, NIV).

My faith is steadfast, anchored in God's promises.

"I live by faith in the Son of God" (Galatians 2:20, NIV).

God's favor surrounds me, paving the way for my dreams.

"I am blessed, for God's goodness surrounds me" (Psalm 23:6, NIV).

I am courageous, pursuing God's plan with boldness.

"I am not afraid, for the Lord is my helper" (Hebrews 13:6, NIV).

I rest in God's faithfulness to fulfill His Word in me.

"I trust God's Word accomplishes His purpose" (Isaiah 55:11, NIV).

I attract God's provision, living in His abundance.

"I am supplied by God's riches in glory" (Philippians 4:19, NIV).

I save wisely, building wealth for God's purposes.

"I gather wealth, for the diligent prosper" (Proverbs 13:4, NIV).

I receive financial breakthroughs aligned with God's will.

"I give, and God pours out blessings I cannot contain" (Malachi 3:10, NIV).

"I am blessed in all I do, for God prospers me" (Deuteronomy 28:8, NIV).

I trust God to provide for every dream He's given me.

My finances are restored by God's redeeming power.

"I recover what was lost, for God restores" (Joel 2:25, NIV).

I manage God's resources wisely, multiplying them.

"I am entrusted with much, for I am faithful" (Luke 16:10, NIV).

I give generously, reaping God's abundant harvest.

"I sow bountifully and reap bountifully" (2 Corinthians 9:6, NIV).

I connect with opportunities that grow my wealth.

"My diligence brings me before kings" (Proverbs 22:29, NIV).

God's prosperity flows through me for His glory.

"I am blessed to be a blessing" (Genesis 12:2, NIV).

I cultivate relationships that honor God and my purpose.

"I choose friends who encourage my faith" (Hebrews 3:13, NIV).

I release unforgiveness, embracing God's freedom.

"I forgive, as the Lord forgave me" (Colossians 3:13, NIV).

I speak blessings over everyone in my life.

"My words build up and give grace" (Ephesians 4:29, NIV).

I connect with divine appointments for my destiny.

"I am led to those God appoints for me" (Psalm 37:23, ESV).

I pray for those who've hurt me, trusting God's plan.

"I pray for those who persecute me" (Matthew 5:44, NIV).

I steward small tasks faithfully, knowing they lead to big victories. "I am faithful in little, and God entrusts me with much" (Luke 16:10, NIV).

I do not have to be perfect to move forward, and I can celebrate my progress as I take steps forward. "Perfect love drives out fear in me" (1 John 4:18, NIV).

I act with consistency, believing God shows up in my faithfulness. "I am faithful in little, and God entrusts me with much" (Luke 16:10, NIV).

I set clear goals, writing my vision to stay focused. "I write the vision and make it plain, that I may run with it" (Habakkuk 2:2, ESV).

I replace doubt with gratitude, focusing on God's goodness. "I give thanks in all circumstances, for this is God's will for me" (1 Thessalonians 5:18, NIV).

I avoid discouragers, choosing bucket fillers who lift me up. "I seek friendships from those who sharpen me as iron sharpens iron" (Proverbs 27:17, NIV).

I declare my great work, refusing to quit despite opposition. "I press on toward the goal for the prize of God's call" (Philippians 3:14, NIV).

I forgive those who've hurt me, freeing my heart for my destiny. "I forgive others, as my Father has forgiven me" (Matthew 6:14, NIV).

I see betrayal as God's setup for my breakthrough, like Joseph did. "I know that God works all things for my good" (Romans 8:28, NIV).

I wield forgiveness as a weapon, destroying the enemy's plans. "I overcome evil with good" (Romans 12:21, NIV).

I visualize my dreams succeeding, like athletes see victory. "I see God's vision for me easily" (Proverbs 29:18, KJV).

I speak life over my dreams, knowing my words shape my reality. "Life and death are in my tongue, and I choose life" (Proverbs 18:21, NIV).

I reimagine my past with God's redemption, creating a new story. "I am transformed by the renewing of my mind" (Romans 12:2, NIV).

MORE ABOUT THE AUTHOR

Melinda lives with her husband, Pieter, in Redding, California. Melinda and Pieter have three grown children, and they live on a mini farm with cats, dogs, goats, and chickens. Melinda's husband Pieter is the founder of Bezalel Innovations, a medical technology company based in Redding, California. They are both licensed pastors at Bethel Church in Redding, California. Melinda and her husband Pieter are passionate about seeing marriages restored and seeing people step into their dreams. Melinda and Pieter's powerful testimony demonstrates that love conquers all and dreams can be resurrected, no matter the circumstance.

OTHER BOOKS BY MELINDA & PIETER LAGAAY

The Supernatural Power of Deliverance, *Experiencing the Blood of Jesus to Set the Captive Free*

Silently Broken, Loudly Restored, *the Radical Power of God's Transforming Love for a Fallen Surgeon*

Made in the USA
Coppell, TX
19 February 2026

71812980R00079